THE NINETEEN HUNDREDS

STONY STRATFORD CELEBRATES THE DIAMOND JUBILEE OF 1897

Stony Stratford was gaily bedecked for this occasion. The Rising Sun was rebuilt in 1742, and just beyond it was a disreputable group of houses known as Parker's Yard, which was demolished in the 1930's. In the group of boys can be seen (second from right) Mr. W. J. Toms, Headmaster for many years of Stony Stratford Senior School. The floppy hats of the little girls are typical of the period. *See page 10*

THE
NINETEEN HUNDREDS

being the story of

the Buckinghamshire towns of

WOLVERTON

AND

STONY STRATFORD

during the years 1900—1911

BY

S. F. MARKHAM, M.A., B.Litt., etc.

With drawings and maps by

CHARLES W. GREEN

and other illustrations.

First printed in 1951
by E.N. Hillier & Sons Ltd
Market Hill, Buckingham, Bucks

Reprinted 1991 by
Wolverton & District Archaeological Society

I.S.B.N. 0 9512973 2 5

CONTENTS

ABOUT THE AUTHOR

SYDNEY FRANK MARKHAM (Major Sir Frank Markham, D.L., M.A., B.Litt., Dip. Econ, M.P.) was the second son of the eight children of William and Nellie Markham. His father was a Prudential insurance agent, a parish councillor and the secretary of the Stony Stratford Horticultural Show and the Football club.

Sir Frank was born in 1897, as his birth certificate says "on the Green" in Stony Stratford, but in time the family moved to 58 Wolverton Road, a house with a spacious garden which helped provide for the large family.

His first school was St. Mary's Infants (now the Plough Inn) and then St. Giles Boys' School (now 30-32 High Street). He left school at 14 but continued at "night school" in the Science & Art Institute, Church Street, Wolverton (its site is the car park adjacent to the Agora Centre and St. George's Church). His first job was as a messenger boy for McCorquodale's, Wolverton, then as a junior clerk in the Stony Stratford & Wolverton Tram office, followed by Sharp & Wollards, Church Street, Stony Stratford and then at the Wolverton, London & North Western Railway Works offices. There, in 1915, when he was aged 17, he was recruited into the British Red Cross unit in Bethune, France. Upon reaching 18, he served in the trenches for three years with the Royal West Kents until he won a Commission as the result of a Field exploit.

As an officer in the Oxford & Bucks Light Infantry he served in Ireland and in Mesopotamia (now Iraq) and then with the 11th Rajputs in Chitral.

Excitement seemed to follow him, in his progress from a Private in the First World War to a Staff Officer in the Second. Stationed in Cork in Ireland he escaped death by a sudden change of duties. In India he rode through the Khyber Pass with the mad Fakir of Ipi marauding the countryside, and while seeking White Russian refugees in the Hindu Kush was thrown from his horse over a precipice. He spent three days on the quay at Dunkirk, having collected 800 non-combatants during the retreat, and returned to England in a barge. He was in Knightsbridge Barracks in the blitz; on a quay in Constantine, North Africa when an ammunition ship blew up; he earned his mention in dispatches before Tunis; and in mid-Atlantic, while on a Parliamentary Mission to Australia and New Zealand via New York, his ship was hit by a torpedo. After the Second Front he was on Eisenhower's staff, in military government in Osnabruck and on Luneberg Heath at the Surrender. He won twelve medals and a mention in dispatches.

But to return to 1921, he resigned his commission and entered Oxford University as a Scholar at Wadham, he rowed for his college, spoke in the Oxford Union and gained three degrees.

He then became secretary to Sir Sidney Lee and upon Lee's death was commissioned to finish the official biography of King Edward VII. Other histories followed until he became secretary to the Principal of the London School of Economics, working on a 'Survey of London Life and Labour' for Sir William Beveridge. In 1928 he became secretary to the Museums Report, going on to be secretary to the Association, Empire Secretary and finally President of the Association of the Museums and Art Galleries of Great Britain. He published many world-wide Reports and Directories of Museums for the Carnegie Corporation of New York and a Report on the 'Illiteracy of the Parsees' for the Harkness Trust.

He was elected in 1928 as a Buckinghamshire County Councillor for Wolverton but in his retirement became a Councillor and a Deputy-Lieutenant for Bedfordshire (1966).

In politics he was elected as Labour Member for Rochester & Chatham (1929-31) and became a Parliamentary Private Secretary to the Prime Minister, Ramsay McDonald, and later to the Lord President of the Council. Not fighting the next election he was returned as a National Member for Nottingham South (1935-45) and in turn became unpaid Parliamentary Private Secretary to Winston Churchill and to Churchill's "ginger group" before the 1939 War. He founded, and was Chairman of, the Parliamentary Science Committee (1938-9) and of the Parliamentary and Scientific Committee 1940. Defeated in the Socialist landslide of 1945 after his world-wide activity, he returned to his 'roots' and started writing this book.

A vacancy coming in the Buckingham Division, then the County of Buckinghamshire north of Aylesbury, he was unsuccessful in the 1950 election, but in 1951 defeated Aidan Crawley by 54 votes and stayed the Conservative member for his home area until he retired in 1964.

Well-known and knowing the area so well, living in Stony Stratford, with his three sons and two daughters going to local schools, belonging to numerous clubs and societies, playing tennis, hockey and billiards, he was a "constituency M.P." securing further industry to support our then 'two industry' towns.

In 1953 he was knighted by Queen Elizabeth in her Coronation Honours List on the recommendation of Winston Churchill.

In Westminster he was indefatigable in watching over railwaymen's interests and over our armed forces world-wide. He became Chairman of a senior Parliamentary Defence sub-committee, the House of Commons Select Committee on Estimates, overseeing the finance and organisation of Britain's Sovereign bases throughout the world.

He also headed Parliamentary Delegations to Kenya 1961, Malta, Cyprus & the Mediterranean 1963 and the Far East in 1964.

He was a founder member of the Wolverton & District Archaeological Society and President of the Wolverton and Bletchley Societies.

His publications include:

"Climate and the Energy of Nations " 4th edition USA   1944
"The History of Stony Stratford" (with Professor Hyde)   1948
"The Nineteen Hundreds"   1951
"The History of Milton Keynes & District " Vol I   1973
"The History of Milton Keynes & District "Vol II   1975

He died in October 1975 and is buried in Stony Stratford.

Sir Frank Markham

ILLUSTRATIONS AND MAPS

ILLUSTRATIONS AND MAPS

PREFACE

THE ASTONISHING WELCOME given to " The History of Stony Stratford " three years ago has encouraged me to produce this sequel, for the former ended with the close of the 19th century, and the present book brings the story up to the eve of the first World War.

As will be gathered from the text, the main source of information has been the columns of the *Wolverton Express*, and I should like to thank the Editor, Mr. A. J. Emerton for his assistance in so many ways. The *Bucks Standard* and the other local newspapers, including the defunct *North Bucks Advertiser* and the *Buckingham Express* have also been referred to. All this has provided the basic material for the work, but added to this have been many personal memories, of which my own take perhaps too large a share, but they were the easiest to refer to, and are perhaps excused by the fact that I was born and bred in Stony Stratford, and partly educated in Wolverton. It was in Wolverton also that I found my first employment, and was first elected to public office.

Amongst others who have helped in this pleasantly reminiscent task of looking back I should like to mention Mr. Walter Marsh, for many years a great friend of my father, Mr. H. E. Meacham, Director of Messrs. McCorquodale and Co., who has helped greatly with publication problems, Mr. F. S. Wollard and Mr. T. J. Tibbetts, who might be described as Joint Holders of the Unofficial Mayoralty of Stony Stratford, the Misses Maguire and Miss Plumb, Mrs. Cowley, Dr. Douglas Bull and Mr. E. W. Russell, of Stony Stratford, Mrs. Watts, Mr. E. W. Compton, Mr. T. Dickens, Mr. E. C. Turvey and Mr. H. Swain, of Wolverton ; Mr. A. J. Negus of Yardley Gobion, Mr. E. F. Instone of New Bradwell, Mr. W. R. Mitchell of Newport Pagnell, Mr. E. T. Ray of Bletchley and Mr. L. Wulcko. Many others I should like to thank for the loan of photographs (their names are given beneath the illustrations) and for the gift of corroborative detail. I am also indebted to Mr. R. Staley for help in the preparation of the typescript.

Finally, my warmest thanks are due to my friend from school days, Mr. C. W. Green, for his advice on many matters and for his mastery of the graphic art that adds so much to the attractiveness of this book.

I need scarcely add that for the many imperfections of this book I am alone responsible, and I must confess that as one looks back the mind seems to play many tricks. Then, the sun seemed brighter, there was a glow in the air and novelty in everything ; fields and houses and shops were certainly larger, and without question everybody was much more of an individual than many seem to be to-day. But all these illusions are perhaps a sure sign that I have reached middle age, and therefore have become fallible in judgment and memory, but not, I hope deficient in kindliness in describing events and personalities in the Nineteen Hundreds.

S. F. MARKHAM.

July 1951.

CHAPTER I

The Decade Opens

IF WE TAKE A MAP of England and Wales and endeavour to find the areas furthest from the sea, one of those areas will certainly be that which includes South Northants and North Bucks. It is not a spectacular area, for it consists mostly of the gentle farming lands bordering the Great Ouse as it runs between Buckingham and Newport Pagnell. It is a land almost unknown to trippers and tourists, and indeed far removed from anything but English influences. In the middle of this area lie the two towns of Stony Stratford and Wolverton, which are as great in contrast perhaps as any two small towns within two miles of one another as can be found anywhere. When the Romans made their great Watling Street, Stony Stratford marked the point where that important artery crossed the only fair sized river between London and Chester. Saxons, Normans, Plantagenets and Yorkists helped to develop the area ; and in the times of the Civil War it was often in the no-man's land between Parliamentary and Royalist forces. In the great coaching days it was a most important stop on the London-Manchester run. When, in 1838, the railway engineers made the iron road from London to Birmingham, Wolverton, and later New Bradwell, came into being, as typical industrial towns.

Around these two towns lie the historic and beautiful villages of Passenham, Calverton, Potterspury, Old Bradwell, Wicken and Cosgrove, a little further off lie the ancient market towns of Buckingham and Newport Pagnell, and the newer town of Bletchley.

It is of this area that we tell our tale, and the period chosen, like the country, is one of the most peaceful in all England, for the decade 1900—1910 was one when Europe was at peace. It was an era when Britain still ruled the waves, when life and prices were stable. This, therefore, is no heroic history of battles or sieges, of catastrophic change, of famine or plague, but a history of two small English towns and their surrounding villages in a time of almost perfect peace.

THE BOER WAR

Yet it was not exactly perfect peace, for during the period 1870 to 1900 British troops had fought in over a hundred faraway wars and frontier engagements against Zulus, Dacoits, Pathans, Dervishes, and many other tribes whose valour was equal to ours, but not their artillery. The army in those days was entirely a volunteer army, and one of the colourful displays in our own countryside were the chromatic posters outside police stations advertising the army, and the visits of the equally colourful recruiting sergeant with ribbons in his cap and shillings in his pocket.

Yet in spite of British valour, the British army was sadly lacking somewhere when it came up against a foe with guns and horsemanship equal to its own. South Africa had been a succession of tragedies. Majuba Hill, during the first Boer War, had proved that the farmer Boers could out-general us, and the opening months of the second Boer War which began on October 10th, 1899, were even less auspicious. In the Black December of 1899 a series of British defeats by the Boers were startling, and the country suddenly learnt that the Boers were neither Dacoits, nor Zulus, nor Dervishes. An appeal was made for more troops. The call was answered well, and from Stony Stratford, Wolverton, Buckingham, and Newport Pagnell, hundreds of men, already in the Volunteers, volunteered for South Africa.

On the 1st January 1900 a meeting was held at the Science and Art Institute when it was announced that no less than 86 members of the Wolverton Rifle Volunteers had volunteered for service in South Africa. Their names are given in Ratcliff's History of the Newport Hundreds, p. 291-2. Five weeks later, on February 6th, a farewell dinner was given to those selected to serve, and the scene of loyalty and enthusiasm was indescribable. The following morning they paraded on the Market Square under the command of Major Williams and Lieutenant Hawkins, and marched off to the Railway Station headed by the band playing the regimental quick step " Ninety Five ".

This was but one local group in one local company and there were many others who answered their country's call.

Most of those who went from this area arrived in South Africa early in 1900, about the same time as Lord Roberts and Lord Kitchener were beginning to turn the tide of defeat into victory. The Siege of Kimberley was raised on February 15th, and twelve days later the Boer General Kronje surrendered with 4,000 Boers at Paardeberg. The next day Ladysmith was relieved. On March 13th Bloemfontein, the capital of the Orange Free State was taken by Lord Roberts, and on May 17th Mafeking was relieved. This swift succession of victories was welcomed at home ; but in an odd way none with greater enthusiasm and idiotic caperings than the Relief of Mafeking, where Colonel Robert Baden-Powell and his small inventive band had been shut up since the previous November. At Wolverton the news was received with such acclaim that gangs of youths went cheering, singing and shouting about all over the Works, and such was the general inclination to celebrate that all work had to be suspended for the day, bonfires were lit at night, oxen were roasted whole, and the public houses did a roaring trade.

Wolverton was not satisfied with mafficking around on that one day alone, for the following Saturday, the 19th May was given over to celebrations as well. But even this was not sufficient, and on the following Saturday an extra demonstration was organised for the benefit of the 1,300 school children of the town. There were the usual concomitants of a procession with the band, a tea, presentation of medals, and so on ; but there were unusual items like a maxim gun, lent by Major Williams, which was drawn by boys, and several horsemen in costume amongst whom could be recognised Mr. John Eady made up to represent Lord Roberts in full regimentals. Mr. Charles Bonsor represented Major General Baden-Powell, whilst Mr. Thomas Eady and Mr. Ernest Walton represented the New South Wales Lancers. It is a great regret that I cannot illustrate this passage with a picture of Mr. Eady as Lord Roberts, for it must have been a truly remarkable portrayal.

On June 5th, 1900, Lord Roberts entered Pretoria, the capital of the Transvaal, and in the following November, having decided that the war was virtually over, returned to England. But the commando Boers, under Generals de Wet and Jan Smuts, had not realised this, and for another 18 months they kept the British troops very bewildered and baffled by their forays and excursions.

In Stony Stratford and Wolverton everybody knew what Lord Roberts or Lord Kitchener looked like, for all the boys wore patriotic buttons with their portraits upon them ; and even the round-a-bouts, the switchbacks and the ice-cream barrows had colourful portraits not only of these two leaders, but also of General French, who had relatives at Hanslope Park and often stayed there, and Major General Baden-Powell.

Our local men who had gone out to the South African War went out in two main groups, the one from Stony Stratford with the Bearer Company, Home Counties Volunteer Infantry Brigade, and the other from Wolverton and Stony Stratford with the 1st Bucks Rifle Volunteer Corps, but in addition to these there were others, principally from Newport Pagnell and Buckingham who had been in the Royal Bucks Hussars or Bucks Yeomanry.

The Wolverton Company (No. 6) of the 1st Bucks R.V.C. had been formed in 1877, and the first recruit was Mr. T. Pooley, of Wolverton, who later became Colour Sergeant. At the beginning of the Boer War the Company was commanded by Major H. M. Williams, who had also joined in 1877 and had won rapid promotion, and Mr. L. C. Hawkins was a subaltern. It was the latter who led the contingent of 40 from Wolverton to South Africa (the full list of those who served is engraved on a brass shield to be seen in the Science and Art Institute). The Stony Stratford Company (No. 7) was formed about 1881 when its headquarters were at the Old St. Paul's College. One of the earliest to join was Mr. W. L. Marsh, who became a sergeant in 1893 (subsequently Captain in World War I), who from the first showed a rare prowess in shooting, and in the 1900's became one of the most renowned shots in the County.

In addition to the Stony Stratford Company of the 1st Bucks Volunteer Corps (which was transferred to Wolverton in 1904), there was also the Bearer Company (later R.A.M.C.) which had been formed by Dr. (later Colonel) W. H. Bull around 1880, and had its headquarters at the Cock Hotel. It was part of the Home Counties Volunteer Brigade, of which no less than 35 per cent. volunteered for service in South Africa. All the Stratford men returned except Sergeant Cherry, who, it was said, had got a very good appointment at Pretoria.

It cannot be out of place to record briefly the experiences of some of these men. When, for example, the call for more volunteers for South Africa went out in January 1900, Mr. David Meakins, a fine figure of a man and a member of the Stony Stratford Fire Brigade, promptly volunteered for service

STONY STRATFORD'S BOER WAR HERO

Photograph lent by Mr. Fred Downing

Trumpeter Frank Downing, who won the Distinguished Conduct Medal in the South African War when only 18 years of age. The photograph was taken just before he left for South Africa, outside John Attwood Reeve's stables (now the Picture Palace). In the background can be seen the White House. For the story of his exploit see p. 5.

VOLUNTEERS IN CAMP AT SHORNCLIFFE, 1900

Photograph lent by Mr. J. Ibell

The photograph was taken in August 1900 during the annual camp of the Stony Stratford contingent of the Bearer Company, Home Counties Volunteer Infantry Brigade. Standing at the back are Corporal H. Tucker and Privates W. Wood and F. Bradbury who had just come off guard duty. Seated with the mallet is Pte. J. Pratt, and in front (l. to r.) Pte. J. West, Bugler J. O. Ibell and Pte. H. Pitt. See pp. 4 and 136.

Block lent by the Wolverton Express

THE RETURN OF THE VOLUNTEERS FROM THE SOUTH AFRICAN WAR

One of the remarkable features of the period was the enthusiastic welcome given to returning heroes from the South African War. Our photograph shows a crowd at Wolverton Station awaiting their arrival. See p. 8.

with a field ambulance to accompany the Imperial Yeomanry, and Ptes. Flint, Ogden, Grant, Felts, Galtress and Mould, of the 1st Bucks also volunteered in a group. Within a few weeks all were out in South Africa. Mr. Meakins found himself attached to the Imperial Yeomanry Base Hospital at Delfontein, which then had about 200 patients for 700 beds. Many of the beds had been provided by local subscriptions : there was a " Stony Stratford and Calverton Bed ", two " Wolverton Beds ", and a " Newport Pagnell Bed ". Of the casulaties, there were twice as many cases of sickness as of battle wounds : enteric fever was in fact the greatest foe, but scarlet fever and dysentry were frequent too. Whilst in Delfontein Mr. Meakins saw Kronje and his defeated troops coming through as prisoners : and also Trumpeter Frank Downing, of Stony Stratford, as one of their guards. A few months later the 18-year-old Trumpeter, who was the son of Q.M. George Downing, of Stony Stratford, and was now serving with the Imperial Yeomanry, found himself in a most exciting incident, and here is his own description of it as written in simple language to his younger brother, Harry, aged 11 :—

Kroonstaad, O.R.C.,
Nov. 9th, 1900.

Dear Harry,

    I am writing this letter to you though I hope you will let father and mother see it. We have had some very wet weather this last fortnight ; we had heavy rain one night, we were camped on a flat piece of ground, and before morning we were standing in six inches of water. I sat in a Cape cart all night with the tilt up, and blankets and saddles were floating everywhere. We marched next morning, you never saw such a sight in your life. We went to try and get those Berks Volunteers that were captured at Ventersburg. We went to Ventersburg Road and stayed there till 12 p.m. then marched on to Ventersburg. We were the advance guard, and General Hamilton rode with us and was talking to us. We reached the town just at daybreak, and we ran right into the sleeping Boers, who fled, leaving their clothes behind them. We had an awful fight, and the Major of the Artillery was killed. We took a kopje and held it, and the Lancers (9th and 16th) thought we were Boers, and were shooting at us for half an hour, but did not hit us. We had some fine shots at the Boers, who had a lot of boys with them. That night it began to rain, and kept on for forty hours without ceasing once. Fancy, no roof over us but the sky, and no tents. When it stopped raining we burnt half the town down and marched in a roundabout way to Kroonstaad. Only the mounted troops came with us. The infantry went by rail. There were the Remington Tigers, ourselves, and some mounted infantry details, with three guns of the 39th batallion under Colonel Remington. We were advancing on the extreme flank when we heard shots. The mounted infantry were at a farm, burning it and were attacked by about 200 Boers. We galloped up and held the farm whilst they retired. Then they took up a position and held it whilst we retired. We were only about one to three Boers, and had seven miles to go before we could get re-inforcements. We had to retire in turns, like I explained. One of the mounted infantry got his horse shot, and was left behind before anybody saw him, I rode back for him and got him up behind me, and then had a race with three Boers, but the English horse, though he had two on his back, won easily. They got within 200 yards of me and whilst I was getting on, the bullets began to come very close. Then, to make matters worse, the mounted infantry opened fire on us, not knowing who it was. When I had nearly reached our men they began to retire, one stood up and fired point blank at me before he saw who it was. I had about a mile and a half to gallop altogether before I was out of range, and Mr. Ricardo came down and broke his collar bone during the gallop. When I got in camp Colonel Remington sent for me, and congratulated me, and then he sent in a recommendation for the Distinguished Service Medal for me ; he sent it to General Hamilton, who said he would do all he could for me. If I get it I shall not have done so badly. We are now left with Mr. Shepherd Cross in command of two companies ; all the other officers have gone home and left us to it. I hope to spend Christmas Day with you. Love to all. I remain, Your loving Brother,

FRANK G. DOWNING.

Trumpeter 57th Company, Imperial Yeomanry.

P.S. Give the stamp enclosed to Grace, tell her it came out of ex-President Steyn's pocket book, which he left behind when surprised near Bloemfontein.

Five months later Stony Stratford learnt with joy that the young Trumpeter had been awarded the Distinguished Conduct Medal " for bravery in rescuing a wounded trooper whilst under the fire of the enemy ".

In the following June the 56th and 57th Companies of the Imperial Yeomanry returned to England from South Africa. Among them was Frank Downing, and Stratford determined to welcome him as well as ever it could. But first the Yeomanry were welcomed at Southampton and then 75 of them came on to Buckingham for a magnificent reception at the Town Hall, where the Royal Bucks Hussars, the Mayor and Corporation, and so on, welcomed them royally. Finally the young trumpeter managed to get away, and found his father, the Quarter Master of the Royal Bucks Hussars, ready to drive him to Stratford.

Meanwhile at 8 p.m. the Stratford Town Band (under Mr. T. Sharpe), the Church Lads Brigade (under Captain the Rev. H. C. Izard) and a truly astonishing crowd assembled at the bridge over the Ouse. After a long wait the wagonette was hailed, careering along escorted by a troop of Hussars. Then the cheering started. The horses were taken out of the shafts, young Harry and other immediate friends clambered aboard and scores of sturdy townsmen took turns when they could to pull the chariot along. At the Barley Mow Inn a little order was restored, and a proper procession formed. The Royal Bucks Hussars led with drawn swords, then came the band and the Church Lads Brigade, and finally the wagonette with the young hero grinning cheerfully at everybody.

In the midst of all the din Doctor W. H. Bull, Chairman of the Reception Committee was believed to have made a short speech of congratulation and welcome, and then the band struck up with " Welcome Home " and everybody cheered and cheered for the whole length of the High Street, until at last at the corner of London Road, where the Downing home was, suddenly everybody was quiet. The calls for a speech from ' young Frank ' were to be answered. " I want to thank you for the very hearty reception you have given me. I simply went to South Africa to do my duty, and did not expect any such honour as you have bestowed on me this night. Thank you one and all ". Somebody struck up " For He's a Jolly Good Fellow "—and the band joined in. " The King " follow-ed, and at last everybody went home to bed thoroughly happy.

Such a reception was not reserved for Frank Downing alone, for every South African warrior was a hero whether he had won a medal or not, and during the next few months there were a score of the warm welcomes for returning " Gentlemen in Khaki ".

Mr. Meakins, for example, returned in March 1901, and it is worth while quoting the style of his reception from the *North Bucks Advertiser* of March 15th 1901, which said :—

A very hearty reception was extended to Mr. David Meakins, eldest son of Mr. T. C. Meakins, of High Street, on his arrival in the town on Saturday evening last from South Africa. He arrived at Wolverton by the 7.31 p.m. train, and was met at the railway station by the members of the Stony Stratford Fire Brigade, under Capt. Geo. Downing, with the Fire Engine (Mr. Meakins being a member of the Brigade) and a large circle of friends. On arriving at Stony Stratford, a procession was formed, and headed by the Stony Stratford Brass Band (under the con-ductorship of Mr. Sharpe), Mr. Meakins was escorted in triumph to his home amid the loud cheering of the spectators who lined the roadway. Six peals of grandsire doubles were rung on the Parish Church bells, under the conductorship of Mr. R. Valentine. On arrival at his home in High Street, Stony Stratford, Mr. Meakins returned thanks for the hearty reception accorded him. Amongst the many who extended to him a cordial welcome home were the Vicar (Rev. J. H. Light), and Brigade-Surgeon Lieut.-Col. Bull.

Mr. Meakins has brought home with him a capital collection of curios and war trophies, including skins of wild animals, Kaffir bangles, Kruger coins, Boer tobacco, pipe and razor, native embroidery, Pom-Pom shell, fragments of shell and shrapnel which were fired into Ladysmith, and other interesting relics.

Two months later, on May 18th 1901, the men of the Wolverton Volunteers returned and seldom had the area seen a greater display of decorations and patriotic feeling than when they arrived home. Previously they had been met at High Wycombe by the Mayor and Corporation and the officers of the 1st Bucks Battalion, where, after divine service they were all entertained to lunch, after which the section entrained for Wolverton. The arrival of the special train at Wolverton was heralded by fog signals and deafening cheers. A procession was then formed and marched to the church, after which everybody marched to the Market Square. Here Mr. C. A. Park, Superintendent of the Works addressed Lieutenant Hawkins and the men in words that deserve to be quoted, for after welcoming them all back he said :—

The only thing I think we perhaps regret, and no one regrets it more than yourselves, is that you had not the opportunity of doing a little more fighting. Still, you have done your work and your duty nobly and well. There must, of course, be some to guard the lines of communication, and you have done your work like true Britons . . .

But two Wolvertonians did not return from South Africa, and in the Cemetery there is a simple obelisk to the memory of Private J. M. Gould " the first Bucks Volunteer to die on Active Service in the South African Campaign ", and to Trooper G. Ruddlesden, formerly of Wolverton, who was killed in action at Krugersdorp in September 1900.

It was not until nearly 18 months after the return of the Wolverton Volunteers that an event occurred which was actually received with great calm. On May 31, 1902 peace was signed at Vereeniging, in South Africa, which thus brought to a close the Boer War. Two years earlier, when the news came through that Mafeking had been relieved both Wolverton and Stony Stratford went delirious. But when peace was actually signed, as the *Wolverton Express* primly remarks :—

The officials of the L.N.W.Ry. saw to it that there was no repetition of the scenes that marked the Relief of Mafeking, when bands of youths paraded the Works shouting and singing until work stopped in confusion, but at 9.40 a.m. the hooter blew. Impromptu processions, headed by the band of the Wolverton Detachment, 1st Bucks Rifle Volunteer Corps, (Bandmaster Brooks) paraded the town playing " Soldiers of the Queen " and other popular tunes.

Once the war was over, plans were swiftly put into effect for the return of the rest of the troops, and they returned almost in the same groups as they went out. Thus every village and town in the country had one great occasion on which to welcome home the heroes of the veldt.

On July 12th 1902, six from Bradwell who had served out there with the 1st Bucks Royal Volunteer Corps were welcomed home. All was carefully arranged. The Band met them at the station, and played them home to the tunes of " The C.I.V. March ", " When Johnny Comes Marching Home Again ", and of course " Dolly Grey " and " Goodbye, My Bluebell", which were anything but homecoming tunes, but they were the rage and that was that. The homecoming of these heroes of the South African War was quite different from anything that happened after the first and second world wars, since, for the South African War, most units were raised on a territorial (county) basis, it followed that the local heroes " Who've been, me lad, who've seen, me lad ", came home in one bunch ; and the localities saw to it that they were properly welcomed and fêted.

At Stony Stratford a special " Welcome Home " Fund was formed, and £83 collected. With this, ten " gold watches and cases " were bought, and a formal presentation made at a superb dinner held in the Cock Hotel. Of those who then went out to South Africa, whether with the Imperial Yeomanry, the Volunteers, or the Brigade Bearer Company, two at least are still alive, Sergeant Beard and Frank Downing, who can show the gold watches presented by the grateful townspeople of Stony Stratford.

After all, it was not such a bad war. It had been fought very far away from England, and though it had lasted longer than expected, there had been remarkably few battle casualties ; in fact every man from Wolverton and Stony Stratford, bar two, had returned, looking bronzed and fit, as heroes should, but which was more due to the sunshine of South Africa than any particular heroism.

In addition to this, thousands of square miles had been added to the Empire, the disaster of Majuba had been avenged, and perhaps most of all, the war had shown the solidarity of the Empire, for contingents from Canada, Australia and New Zealand had fought alongside our own. And Ireland had been splendid too.

It is almost impossible to recapture the spirit of the time. There was still a great faith in Britain's destiny, we were still the greatest nation in the world, we had built up an empire greater than Caesar or Charlemagne or Napoleon could have imagined, and we had done it all from a little island with less than 40,000,000 people. Perhaps even more than all this we had taught the world the integrity of British justice, the value of British goods, we had invented and distributed to the world the railway ; in every field British scientists led, British manufacture triumphed. The Englishman of the 1900's can be forgiven if he felt sometimes that God really meant us to inherit the earth and to bring Christianity and trade to the furthermost parts thereof.

The cheering for the returned heroes had barely died away when there was another great occasion for public rejoicing, and that was the Coronation of Edward VII. The Coronation had been planned for June, but just before the appointed time the King was found to be suffering from appendicitis, which few up to then had ever heard of, but which for years afterwards was a very fashionable complaint. The postponed Coronation was arranged for August 9th, and local Committees of all the local notabilities set out to arrange an attractive programme. At Stony Stratford they not unnaturally considered what had happened at the Diamond Jubilee of Queen Victoria in 1897, only five years earlier, and it may not be out of place to recall the festivities on that occasion.

THE DIAMOND JUBILEE

It is difficult in these days to imagine the outburst of loyalty —the patriotic fervour—which characterised the Diamond Jubilee of Queen Victoria. To have reigned for 60 years was in itself an achievement, and when such a reign had been accompanied by a growing strength and prosperity for the whole nation there was genuine reason for jubilation. But there was something more than this, a real feeling of affection for the little grey-haired widow of Windsor. At Wolverton many had seen her in person, for in the old days Wolverton had been a compulsory refreshment stop for all the more important trains, and many times had the Queen stepped out of the royal train and enjoyed the hospitality of Wolverton Station.

Throughout the whole of this area every possible preparation was made to celebrate the Diamond Jubilee royally—yet looking back it is astonishing how little they had with which to celebrate. There were, of course, the local bands, the bell-ringers, the usual number of people who could sing or recite, or run and jump, but nothing really spectacular. Therefore when we consider how this locality celebrated the Diamond Jubilee it must be judged against a background of very limited united endeavour.

At Stony Stratford a Committee was formed of all the Parish Councillors, and soon the plans were ready, but not until there had been a fierce debate as to whether it was better to give the children and old persons a treat or to have an illuminated clock. The children won the day.

When, on Sunday, June 20th 1897, Diamond Jubilee Day began, not with the dawn, but the moment midnight had sounded, the bells crashed out merrily. Early in the morning finishing touches were put to the dozen or so of streamers across the High Street or to the many lurid decorations of shops or private houses. The streamers all had short messages, which varied from " 60 not out " and " All hearts are glad and bright ", to the sober and scholarly " Victoria Regina " provided by Mr. Odell. Chinese lanterns and fairy lights were all in readiness. In the morning there was a church parade at St. Giles, with Colour-Sergeant Elmes leading the Stony Stratford Company of the 1st Bucks Volunteers, and Sergeant Major West leading the Medical Staff Corps. The Fire Brigade in full dress uniform were there too, and every scholar and most of the grown-ups. Then, after church, came the procession all around the town, and the final dismissal at St. Oswalds House, the residence of Lieut.-Col. W. H. Bull.

On the Tuesday the real fun and games began. Early in the morning some enthusiasts fired the anvils in a royal salute on the Green—a proceeding of some danger to all concerned. Then everybody who could strolled around the town admiring the decorations, and the church bells rang again. Meanwhile the Band, accompanied by cyclists in fancy dress paraded the town. In the afternoon a thousand people gathered in the Market Square ; the children were there, all being marshalled for the procession, the Friendly Societies were there with banner and sashes, and what with the Band and the Fire Brigade and everybody else, the procession was nearly half a mile in length. Finally everybody was shepherded into position, and off they went by Silver Street to the Green, Wolverton Road and down the High Street to the College Field, where they arrived just in time for tea. What a tea! The quadrangle of the old College was full with 850 children, the 120 old people had their meat tea in the Dining Hall, and the remaining thousand inhabitants of the old town either helped serve, carve, or distribute the commemoration Jubilee mugs, oranges and buns, or got ready for the sports that were to follow.

There were 18 events, all just what one would expect, with the exception that the various Parish Councils were supposed to provide tug-of-war teams from their Councillors, but who, perhaps on account of the tea or the sun, felt quite unable to line up. There were games in plenty, including " Kiss in the Ring ", and scrambles for nuts and sweets for the children.

At ten o'clock all had to go home, and everybody agreed that for a Diamond Jubilee it was not so bad.

Although the town did not get its illuminated clock as a memorial to the Queen, it gained by another memorial, a Drinking Fountain (for horses and men) by the Congregational Church. The Drinking Fountain only lasted 30 years, when it was ruthlessly dumped on the scrap heap by a Council which had forgotten both Queen Victoria and the horses.

On January 22nd, 1901, Queen Victoria died. The event was not by any means unexpected, for she was over 80 years of age, but all the same it shocked all England. There were very few living then who could remember any other sovereign but Queen Victoria, who had reigned for 64 years. One of the oddest things is that for not just months, but years afterwards people still sang " God Save the Queen " : it was very hard indeed to get used to the fact that Edward VII was now King.

At Wolverton the news of the Queen's death was received with the same almost silent confusion as in most parts of Britain. " The Queen is dead " passed from lip to lip, and many paused at work to wonder what the future might now hold. Few could possibly have predicted that the next fifty years would see greater changes in everybody's way of life than had indeed happened during the past two or three centuries. The Victorian era had passed in the night, but it was years before men realised that not only an era had passed, but a way of thinking and living.

STONY STRATFORD CELEBRATES THE CORONATION OF 1902

Crowds gathered early on August 9th, 1902 to wait for the procession that was one of the local ways of rejoicing at the accession of King Edward VII. The old White Horse Inn dates from about 1520, but was rebuilt about 1740. *See page* 13.

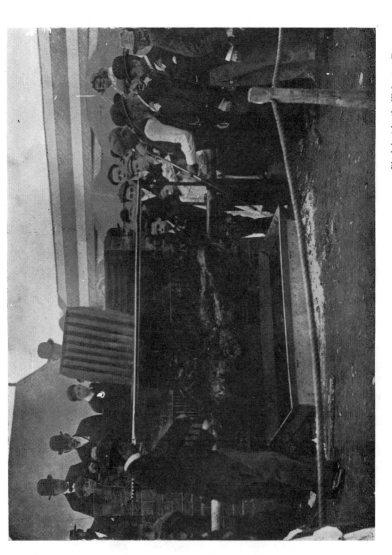

Block lent by the Wolverton Express

WOLVERTON ROASTS AN OX FOR THE CORONATION OF KING EDWARD VII.

On a vacant lot on which is now built the Crauford Arms an ox was roasted in August 1902. Mr. Impey is seen presiding with the ladle. Portions of the roasted ox were distributed to all who brought a plate.

THE CORONATION OF 1902

For the new Coronation the plans were not very different from those of the Diamond Jubilee. At Wolverton the Fire Brigade, the band, the children and all processed around the town, and a tea for the children followed. The most unusual event was the roasting of an entire ox at the corner of Windsor Street and Stratford Road, then a vacant lot, but on which now stands the Craufurd Arms. As can be seen in our illustration there was a little enclosure properly roped off, and inside this Mr. Impey and his colleagues basted and roasted, and roasted and basted until at last the ox was declared fit to be eaten. Then everybody who brought a plate with them was allowed to have a slice, a precaution which effectively prevented stray revellers from Bradwell or Stratford taking part in Wolverton's celebration.

At Stony Stratford there was a similar free tea and treat for the children, but no ox, even though there was a traditional ox-roasting site ready in the Barley Mow field. But among the amusements which Wolverton had not got was the competition of " Climbing the Greasy Pole ". This was a tall scaffold pole liberally greased with soft soap, and as can be imagined the first few efforts were rewarded with great laughter as the grease proved too much for them. Each succeeding effort naturally took more and more grease off. At last the most renowned greasy pole climber in the neighbourhood, Mr. Eli Alderman, popularly known as " Cinder Billy ", judged that the time had come for his effort. His climbing was superb and catlike, cautious and logically deliberate. Not a single slip or slide, for that, he knew, would gather grease, and each foot gained was held without giving an inch. A foot from the top, where a succulent leg of mutton was perched, he paused, and put one hand after the other into his shirt. The cries of encouragement came from all except his competitors, who quite probably were praying for his literal down-slide. Then came the last foot, with the scaffold pole swaying backwards and forwards, and finally he touched, gripped, and won the leg of mutton. A great " A-a-h " from everybody, and then the cheering, with us small boys capering round in delight because we had seen " Cinder Billy " win the leg of mutton. Then we inched up to him, and gazed in awe and wonder at his clothes : from foot to chest he was covered in grease—and then I heard a resentful rival say : " He oughn't to be let to put sawdust in his shirt ". All the same, it was a very good Coronation.

CHAPTER II

Industries, Trades and Markets

"THE WORKS"

Wolverton Works, as many people know, was founded by the old London and Birmingham Railway soon after 1838, when the railway line between those two cities was completed. Wolverton being just about half-way between the two great towns, it was decided that this would be an admirable place for the building and repair of locomotives. The earliest sheds and shops were grouped astride what was then the main line, a little to the west of the present station. To accommodate the 700 employees of that period the Railway authorities built Bury Street, Creed Street, Ledsam Street, Young Street, Gas Street, Drivers Row, and Glyn Square on either side of the Stratford Road. All of these except Gas Street were named after officials of the Company, and the latter after its contiguity to the railway Gas Works. The first station was built overlooking the Park, near what is now the Lamp shop, but soon a larger station was opened just off Glyn Square, and it was at Wolverton station that all trains stopped for ten minutes for refreshment during the middle of the 19th century. The rush and scramble of this ten minute halt can be imagined, and has been colourfully described by more than one writer in the national magazine of the time.

In 1860, some years after the merging of the London and Birmingham Railway into the larger London and North Western Railway Company, it was decided to move the locomotive works to Crewe, and to concentrate the carriage and wagon building at Wolverton. The change-over and expansion took from 1865 to 1877 to complete. Gas Street, Drivers Row and Bury Street continued to exist until about 1885 and Green Lane and Bedford Street marked the southern limits of the town. In the following year Mr. C. A. Park became the Works Superintendent, and for the next twenty years there was a steady policy of expansion, both of the Works and of the town. By 1906 the acreage of the Works had grown from 37 to 80, the number of employees from 2,000 to 4,500, and the town had doubled in size. Oxford Street, Cambridge Street, Windsor Street, Victoria Street, Moon Street, and Osborne Street, were all laid out and mostly built up during this period, but it was no longer the railway which was doing the building, and of the hundreds of houses built during this epoch many were bought (through building societies) by the railway workers themselves. Jersey Road and Western Road were added in 1907-8, and the lovely avenue of trees along Western Road to the Cemetery ruthlessly cut down.

It was the same at New Bradwell, where the whole area between Corner Pin and St. James's Church was now being built over. Old Wolverton, however, remained almost unchanged. Between Wolverton Park and the Vicarage was a picturesque row of thatched cottages, but one or two more modern cottages were still being added to Slated Row. Between Wolverton and Stony Stratford the road wiggled and wavered, and along its whole length ran the tramlines of the Stony Stratford and District Light Railway Company, which carried hundreds of railway workers daily.

Prior to September 1901, the power of the various shops in the works was derived from separate steam engines, or gas engines, but under Mr. Park's direction a central power station was designed, and Wolverton was the first Railway works to adopt electric lighting and driving throughout, and, as the official handbook of the Carriage Works issued in 1907 states : " The Power Station is the finest example of its kind in the United Kingdom ".[1]

The General Offices were rebuilt in 1897, and like the rest of the Works, were then a model of efficiency.

It is a great pity that sufficient space is not available to describe each of the shops in turn, for there was no question about it that in 1906 the Wolverton Works, shop by shop, and offices or station, were among the most efficient in the whole world.

Like the works themselves, the products were of equal efficiency. It was here that the Royal Train was designed and built in 1904 ; it was here that the finest railway saloons were built, and all were finished in the traditional L.N.W.Ry. colours,

[1] I am indebted to Mr. Compton, Moon Street, Wolverton, for the loan of this rare brochure, from which most of the material for this section has been taken.

of Kremnitz white and crimson lake. They represented the highest perfection yet attained in carriage building in England. By contrast with these superb examples, there was kept at Wolverton for many years the original railway coach built for Queen Adelaide by a London firm in 1842-3.

Dining cars, family saloons, travelling Post Offices, Parcel Post vans, Fruit and Milk vans, and the newer rail motor cars were all built at Wolverton.

Wolverton Works not only built and designed carriages and wagons, it also cleaned them, and this was probably the first railway works in England to introduce vacuum cleaning, which replaced, as early as 1901, the hard manual labour involved in beating the upholstery.

It is perhaps not astonishing that at this period, and indeed for many years longer, the worker in the Wolverton Works not only knew that he was working in the most up-to-date works in the country, and produced the finest of all railway rolling stock, but also that he belonged to the finest railway in the world. The permanent way was superb, the trains ran to time save only in foggy or icy weather, the fares were the lowest in Europe, the stations were clean, and often beautifully decorated with miniature gardens or rockeries. The old " North-Western " was the Queen of Railways, the Wolverton railway man knew it, and didn't care if the whole world knew it too.

It may be well to describe in a little further detail the saloons and rail motor cars of the period, since they are illustrated by photographs in this book, and certainly represent the acme of railway construction at the beginning of the 20th century.

There is very little mention in the *Wolverton Express* of this period of the L.N.W.Ry. Works at Wolverton, possibly because they continued the even tenor of their way without strikes, fires, or other major upsets. But on December 18th 1903 there is a short reference to the new saloon carriages " which " have recently been exhibited at Euston, and which may be " attached to the royal train, and represent the very latest " design in railway vehicles. They are from the designs of " Mr. C. A. Park, Carriage Superintendent at Wolverton . . . " The compartments when used for night use, are provided " with brass lacquered bedsteads, and when used for day " service the furnishing is three large lounge easy chairs up- " holstered in green and gold tapestry, one oval centre table in " mahogany, with inlay of tulip wood and satin wood, and two

Photograph lent by Mrs. Bevington

THE ROYAL SALOON AND ITS STAFF AT WOLVERTON ABOUT 1903.

In front of the coach (decorated in the traditional L.N.W.Ry. colours of flake white and crimson lake) may be seen the Stationmaster of Wolverton, the conductor of the train, and the various attendants, most of whom came from Wolverton. See p. 15.

Photograph lent by Miss Maguire

THE OLD TRAM AT DEANSHANGER.

From 1888 to 1926 a steam tramway ran from Stony Stratford to Wolverton, but in the early years the line extended to Deanshanger. The photograph shows the old German engine and the smallest of the carriages halted at Deanshanger in 1890. In the background can be seen the Fox and Hounds Inn and behind it the chimney stack and factory of Messrs. E. & H. Roberts, who produced agricultural machinery for close on a century. See pp. 21 and 25.

Photograph lent by F. S. Woollar

THE OLD TRAM AT STONY STRATFORD

The first engine was of German origin, having been made at Munich ; it continued in use until 1926. See p. 21.

Photograph lent by C. H. Markham

THE TRAM IN DIFFICULTIES

Floods along the Wolverton Road in April 1916 created peculiar difficulties for all kinds of transport.

" folding side tables. The saloons are lighted throughout by
" electroliers in the centre of the roof, and corner ornamented
" bracket lamps ".

RAILWAY MOTOR CARS

In 1905 the L.N.W. Railway tried out a new development
that of railway motor cars. In the March of that year orders
were placed at Wolverton and Crewe for the construction of a
number of motor cars to be worked by steam, and a few months
later a few initial experiments were made on the Wolverton—
Newport Pagnell line, and also on the Bletchley—Bedford line.
The new cars were designed to carry 48 passengers, and could
be driven from either end, the passenger entrance being in the
centre. The crew consisted of a driver, stoker and guard, the
latter accoutred with a bell punch to enable him to issue tickets
in the car instead of the usual practice of getting them before-
hand at the Booking offices. One of the features of the new
service was that these steam motor cars could stop at level
crossings to put down and pick up passengers. For some
reason or other, however, the experiments were not a success,
and we hear little about these steam motor cars after a year or
two.

At this period many railway workers belonged to the Amalgamated Society of Railway Servants, later to be fused into the
N.U.R. One of the most interesting features of its activities in
these days was the Annual Parade, when in conjunction with
other Friendly Societies, the great banners were unfurled, and
the various members, accompanied both by the Bradwell and
the Bletchley bands, paraded the streets of Wolverton.

One of the most interesting opinions on the Wolverton
London and North Western Railway Works about this period
comes from an American journalist who visited the Works
early in 1908, and thus recorded his impressions in the *New
York Herald* (Paris edition) in May. He was very impressed
by the royal train, which he agreed was the best in the country ;
then he asked Mr. C. A. Park : " You have no labour troubles,
have you ? " " None ", he answered, " Why should we ? The
men live here in their homes and do not want to go away.
Strikes are out of the question with us. We pay everybody for
what he does. The better men get the better pay, the less
efficient the poorer pay. Everything is piecework. They are
contented, happy, well paid, and prosperous ".

The journalist thought Mr. Park had the American spirit of enthusiasm, push and persistency, and described him as : " keen eyed, good natured, and the men love him ".

Finally the American visited the men at dinner, and has left it on record that one dish in particular appealed to him, as a New Englander, which he had not been able to get in the better restaurants in London, it was fried salt pork and baked potatoes !

Two years later, in March 1910, the rumour swept through the Works that Mr. Park was leaving. Some said he was to be " sacked ", which astonished all who knew and loved this soldierly figure. Rumour soon became more specific, and it was that he had been ordered up to London for " interview ". Somehow even the time of the train he was taking became known, and by 9.30 a.m. that day almost the entire staff crowded on to the Railway Station or lined the Canal banks, and as the train moved out there were cheers of sympathy and the singing of " For he's a jolly good fellow ". But the demonstration did not deflect the blow, and six weeks later Mr. Park retired. He had been Superintendent for 24 years—years that had seen Wolverton almost double in size. The *Wolverton Express*, sensing the public loss, published a special supplement with the photographs of Mr. and Mrs. Park, and a fine description of the presentation to the pair of a gold rose bowl from his former colleagues.

Three months later Mr. Fitzsimons, the Chief Accountant, retired—after 39 years' service at Wolverton. Like Mr. Park he was extremely popular, and their joint retirement, since both families left the area, created a gap which was never filled.

At this period the Works were working a 54-hour week. For most people in Wolverton the morning could be said to begin with " the first hooter ", which went at 5.20 a.m. and was a signal for the general uprising of most of the male population. Work commenced at 6 a.m., with a break at 8.15 for breakfast. Work was resumed at 9 a.m. and continued until 1 p.m. and again from 2 p.m. to 5.30. On Saturdays the hours were 6 to 12, with the usual breakfast interval. Often there was " short time " which meant missing the Saturday morning's work, and the first " quarter " on Monday.

For those who came from Wicken, Nash, Potterspury, Yardley or Beachampton, the day began soon after 4 a.m., for whether one walked, cycled or came by the " Old Mail " it took an hour or more to get to Wolverton. The Old Mail was a wagonette or brake which rumbled its way daily back and forth with its load of working men, and often still carried the mail. Sometimes the men in a village clubbed together to provide their own horse and brake. At Nash for example, £40 was subscribed in this way and the men paid 1/6 per week to be driven backwards and forwards to Wolverton daily. It cost 1/6 per week to stable the horse at the Royal Engineer, Wolverton, and about 4/- per week for stabling and grooming at Nash. The resultant profits paid off the capital.

At Beachampton a Working Men's Van Company was thus formed, and it was run so successfully that they could hold an annual dinner out of the profits.

From Castlethorpe, Bletchley and Newport Pagnell the men came in by special workmen's trains.

The hours were long, yet in spite of this there seemed much more physical energy to spare than there is to-day. On Sundays, when all could have rested, and sports were not yet approved by public opinion, nearly everybody went for a long walk some time during the day. Entire families would go out together on the Sunday afternoon, and it was no uncommon sight to see families of eight or ten all taking their Sunday constitutional.

THE PRINTING AND ENVELOPE WORKS

Wolverton's second industry has been linked with the Railway by birth and association, for in the 1870's the Chairman of the Railway Company—Sir Richard Moon—expressed a desire for a Printing Works to be established here for the employment of the daughters of Wolverton workmen. McCorquodales Works elsewhere had always turned out railway printing, and still do, from the world-famous Bradshaw to the magnificent scenic posters in lithograph, which are the one redeeming feature on our dreary stations.

Accordingly, in 1878, Mr. George McCorquodale, the founder of the firm, opened a small factory for twenty employees, who were engaged in making Registered Envelopes for the G.P.O. On the ordnance map of 1881 we see a little patch of building which was the first one-storey factory. Wolverton then ended abruptly at the " Drum and Monkey ", so the works were well among ploughed fields, but in 1884 and again in 1889, three-storey buildings were added for general printing and binding, cottages erected for the employees and a house built for the

Manager, then Mr. John Appleton. At that time, 120 females and 20 males were employed. About 1890 a Dining Room was opened by Mr. George McCorquodale, the founder of the firm, this being his last visit to Wolverton. Developments of 1894 and 1897 swept away the cottages and Manager's house, just as Bury Street had been engulfed by the L. & N.W.Ry. ; there seems to have been a decided aversion in Wolverton planning to having anybody living on the north side of the road. Early every day the stream of men and girls poured in, from miles around, along muddy roads and canal towing paths. Since entertainment was not as now, laid on like water and gas, everybody made their own fun, so the Printing Works had their own Band ; not perhaps too selective, but they were proud of it, and among their number was young Mr. H. E. Meacham, who was a reputable kettle drummer. They also had their private Fire Brigade, and working hours were occasionally enlivened by trial ' alarms '.

Mr. Appleton was succeeded as Manager by Mr. T. Barrett in 1902, and he by Capt. L. C. Hawkins in 1905. Mr. H. E. Meacham, who had been temporarily transferred to Crewe to assist in new developments there, returned as Assistant Manager, and tremendous expansion began, with which his name has been largely associated. He was to become, in the phrase of Mr. Kenneth McCorquodale " one of the outstanding men in the Printing trade ".

In 1905 the Envelope Department was built, and the whole of the Works re-organised and rearranged. A Power House was erected for generation of current for the much extended need of power and light, and by 1907, 550 men and girls were in employment. It was a great development, but only the prelude to still greater successes. Up to this period, the hours like those on the railway, had been long, and it was McCorquodales, at the recommendation of Mr. Meacham, who first led the way to shorter hours. He pointed out in his report that the early morning shift at 6.30 a.m. might be tolerable for the menfolk, but for the female employees travelling in from around during winter months, it was a hardship which affected health, and consequently output ; with shorter hours better results and happier conditions would inevitably result, which proved to be true. In the September of 1909 they changed the hours to begin at 8 a.m. and finish at 6 p.m. with a dinner-hour break at 12.30. On Saturdays they worked until 1 p.m. In addition to this, contributory pension funds, bonuses for years of service, minimum wage rates, holidays with pay, a mutual sick society and welfare officers were all introduced in later years, and, indeed, McCorquodales could claim (though they never did) that they were not only the best printers and envelope makers in the country, but also among the best employers.

It is pre-eminently a family firm and a family atmosphere is encouraged. Employees of three and four generations in succession are not exceptional, and different branches vie with one another in their boasts of service records, where grandparents teach grandchildren their jobs, and the pensioners come back again to mix socially with their juniors by fifty years.

In 1910, the firm secured a further large Government contract for Postal Stamped Stationery, making necessary another large extension and the influx of a permanent Government staff to supervise and check their stationery. In 1914 Capt. L. C. Hawkins became a Director and went off with the Bucks territorials to the First World War. He was succeeded as Manager by Mr. H. E. Meacham.

THE STEAM TRAM

Leaving Wolverton for the time being, let us take the old tram, which was even then the greatest show-piece of the neighbourhood, and was fascinatingly cumbrous and cumbersome.

In 1885 the " Stony Stratford and District Light Railway Company " was formed. Its Charter allowed the company to run steam trams from Deanshanger, through Old Stratford, Stony Stratford, and Wolverton to Wolverton Cattle Sidings.

The work of laying the rails began in 1886, and the first line was laid from the Barley Mow Inn to Wolverton Station. The original rolling stock consisted of two engines made at Munich, two workmen's cars carrying 120 passengers each (100 seated), one upholstered car seating 80 passengers, a smaller car seating 20 passengers, and four wagons. Two of the wagons or trucks were made with convertible wheels, in order that, when The Cock Hotel was reached, they could be pulled off the lines and around the neighbourhood by horses. In 1889 the route was extended to Deanshanger, the rails running along the left-hand side of the road going to that place, but this branch never paid, and in a year or two was discontinued, but the rails remained for many years. The fare from Wolverton to Deanshanger was 4d., and from Wolverton to Stratford 2d. One of our illustrations shows the old tram near the Fox and Hounds Inn at Deanshanger.

The novelty of travelling to Deanshanger or Wolverton soon wore off and the line settled down to a steady income derived from about 500 workmen, who mostly took weekly tickets at 1s. which entitled them to four rides a day. For many years The Cock Hotel was the Stratford terminus. The company was originally financed by local tradesmen, and Mr. Charles Aveline was the first managing director. He was soon succeeded by Mr. Louis Clovis, who resided at Old Stratford, and whose full name and title, as it was disclosed just before his death, was Prince Louis Lucien Clovis Bonaparte. In 1891 the old Tramway Co. went into liquidation. A new company was formed and Mr. Braggins was the first manager, and the last man in Stratford to wear a top hat daily, for he regarded himself not inferior to a stationmaster, and a top hat was still part of a stationmaster's uniform.

Another personality of the old Tram was " Little Billy " (Mr. Newton), who was less than five feet tall, but of such a robust and jovial nature that he became as famous as the tram itself.

Many stories are told of the old Tram, for its very cumbersomeness meant that it was often off the rails, and this disturbing trait was not infrequently helped by small boys who would fill the tram lines with granite stones which then made up the road surface. The consequent derailment meant much manoeuvring before progress was resumed.

In July 1906 a donkey upset the tram, and itself. One night this unfortunate animal strayed onto the lines near Wolverton, where the hedge then came very close to the tram lines, and on approach of the tram got into the hedge. But as the tram passed the donkey somehow or other got itself caught between the engine and the first car, the donkey was knocked down, and was run over hindwards. The tram was derailed, and all the passengers had to get out and walk to Stratford. The tram happened to be full of a number of boys and girls returning from an outing at Bedford, who gazed awestruck at the struggles of the dying donkey.

We must, however, now leave the tram, for we have arrived in Stony Stratford, which in 1900 was a decaying market town whose glory had passed with the stage-coach and post-chaise.

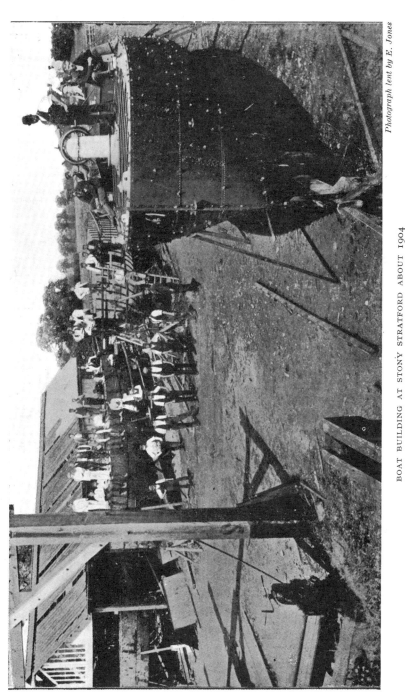

Photograph lent by E. Jones

BOAT BUILDING AT STONY STRATFORD ABOUT 1904

Along the London Road, on the site of what is now the London Road Garage, Messrs. Hayes constructed ocean going craft for over half a century. Our photograph shows four launches or tugs in the course of construction. See p. 23.

TOWING A LAUNCH TO THE CANAL AT OLD STRATFORD

Hayes' Watling Street Works were a mile from the nearest navigable water, so their tugs and launches had to be mounted on a large chassis and towed by steam engine to the Canal at Old Stratford. See p. 23.

Photographs lent by Mr. E. Jones

LAUNCHING AT OLD STRATFORD

The vessel was drawn to the edge of the Canal and then pushed in sideways. From Old Stratford these tugs proceeded along the Grand Junction to London, where they were given the final touches, including the funnel, before going under their own steam to Russia, India or elsewhere. The last launching of this kind was carried out in 1919. See p. 23.

As at Wolverton end there were a few new streets like King
Street, Queen Street and Jubilee Terrace which had been built
a few years since, but with these exceptions the town rejoiced
mainly in 18th century houses, many of which, particularly
along the Green, Silver Street, Horn Lane and the lower end
of the High Street, still had thatched roofs. But even here
plans for rebuilding new streets were being considered. York
Road, Augustus Road, Prospect Road and Coronation Road
were all being planned. Clarence Road had four houses only,
Temperance Terrace had just been built, and Russell Street and
Mill Lane were rapidly being built along. In and about the
town were some disgraceful slums, particularly along the older
inn yards, in the Market Square itself, and near the Gas works
at the Bridge end of the town. Stony Stratford had a curiously
double existence, for whilst probably a third of its adult male
inhabitants worked at Wolverton Works, the remainder owed
their livelihood either to meeting their needs in the retail trades
or to catering for the requirements of the rich agricultural
district which surrounds the town. Public houses and saddlers
throve, whilst the hotels declined, but already the first hoots of
the new-fangled motor car could occasionally be heard up or
down the street, and the old established firm of Hayes, at the
Watling Works, London Road, was forging ahead.

THE WATLING WORKS

In 1840 Edward Hayes, a young engineer from London,
decided to start up in business at Stony Stratford as an agricultural engineer. The firm prospered, and was, indeed, one of
the foremost in Britain for creating and trying out new forms
of machinery to assist the farmer. Now and then there were
enquiries for mechanically driven boats, which led to the firm
specialising in marine engines, and finally, towards the end of
the century, the firm produced vessels ready to go under their
own power to any part of the world. Absence of a broad water
way was no obstacle, for Mr. Edward Hayes Junior and his
staff of eighty found ways and means of launching tugs or
launches nearly 70 ft. long sideways on to the Canal at Old
Stratford, and of manoeuvring them through all the turns and
locks until the Thames was reached. Larger vessels up to 90 ft.
long would be shipped in pieces and assembled on the most
modern pre-fabrication plans.

The reputation of the firm grew as it swept off a number of prizes in international yacht races, tug tests, and so on ; and among those who came to Stony Stratford for tugs or launches were our own Admiralty, the Russian Government, the French Government, the Egyptian Government, and the leading port and dock authorities all over the world. By 1901 the firm was producing twin-screw steam launches 70 ft. in length, 13 ft. 8 in. wide, with a draft of 4 ft., and capable of doing 14 knots ; or stern wheelers 81 ft. 6 in. in length, 14 ft. wide, with a draft of 1 ft. 9 in.

Apprentices were trained, one of whom became Professor Osborne Reynolds, F.R.S., of Manchester, and another, B. J. Fisher, became Chief Engineer of the L. and S.W. Railway, and at least two became presidents of engineering institutions. The late Chairman of Harland and Wolffs, Sir Frederick Rebbeck, was also a pupil of the firm in the nineties. Edward Hayes, Junior, died in 1920, and shortly afterwards the premises became the London Road Garage.

Our illustrations show the type of vessel this enterprising firm created and the ingenious method of launching used in 1906. The vessel was a twin-screw steelplated tug destined for the Nile, and was still doing duty there in the 1940's.

To-day the wharf at Old Stratford is derelict and there is but a fading memory of its past activity, nevertheless, during its prime this firm, eighty miles from the sea, could produce sea-going craft that could challenge the tug-builders of the entire world and often beat them at their own game. Such a vessel would tow 500 tons at 11 m.p.h.

Another old established firm was (and is) that of Messrs. Sharp and Woollard at Stony Stratford. From the Tudor period there had been tanners and leather sellers in the town, and in 1819 the business was bought by Samuel Sharp of Towcester. In the 1850's Mr. F. W. Woollard joined the firm from London, and the business was expanded to include curry-ing. In the 1900's the firm of Sharp and Woollard was re-nowned as one of the most celebrated leather-dressing establish-ments in the Midlands, and remains, with its long ancestry, the oldest established industry in the town. The town still has some of its early account books of the early nineteenth century, and in one at least of these are ancient recipes for leather dressing which are most interesting and peculiar to modern ideas. There was at that time no easy supply of ammonia, and the deficiency was made up by having tubs for the use of the men in convenient places, and utilising the product for the ammonia it contained. In the recipes this ingredient is described as " stale". From all accounts it certainly was.

DEANSHANGER IRON WORKS

Just over two miles from Stony Stratford, at Deanshanger, there were the agricultural machinery works of Messrs. E. & H. Roberts, which had been established in 1820. For nearly a century its ploughs and other agricultural machinery were famous throughout England, and particularly through the Midlands. The firm received a severe blow in 1907 when the senior partner, Mr. Edwin Roberts died, but even more severe blows were to follow, for in that year, England saw one of the first demonstrations of motor tractors and combine harvesters, in Lincolnshire, reported fully in the local press, and after the first world war the motor tractor came to stay, and Messrs. E. & H. Roberts somehow never managed to meet the new conditions.

Another old established industry in the area was, and still is, Cowleys Parchment Works at Newport Pagnell. It is intriguing to know that this ancient industry was first established at Newport in the 17th century, and still produces exquisite parchments, not only for illuminated addresses and scrolls, but also for lamp shades and even for medical purposes.

WAGES AND PRICES

At this period the wages of a craftsman in the Works were about 28s. a week, plus a bonus in certain shops. Unskilled labourers earned 6d. an hour. In the countryside wages were lower, in some cases as low as 12s. a week. But then as now the test was what would the money buy, and by that standard we may come to far different conclusions than these figures give one at first sight. To begin with, the wage was clear income ; there were no deductions for P.A.Y.E., national insurance or national health ; trade union levies were very light, and in general what a man earned he found in his pocket at the end of the week. Even where income tax was paid it was only at the rate of 9d. in the £, and there were neither purchase taxes, entertainment taxes nor pools tax.

Prices in those days were enormously different from what they are to-day ; here, for example, are clothing items taken from the advertisement columns of the local papers for the period 1900—1910 :—

Men's Shirts ...	...	2/11	Blue serge or tweed suits		
Men's Socks ...	...	1/- pr.	to measure	... ...	30/-
Boots (calf leather) ...		8/11 pr.	Overcoats	... 14/11 to 25/-	
Kid gloves ...	1/3 to 2/11 pr.		Ladies Skirts	... 2/11¾ to 3/11½	
Woollen Gloves 5d. to 2/3 pr.			Handkerchiefs	...	1/6 dozen

Food was less frequently advertised, and these are the only items which appear :—

Bread	...	5d. quartern loaf	Currants ...	...	3d. per lb.
Flour ...	...	... 10d. gallon	Dates	... ...	2d. per lb.

Perhaps the greatest changes are to be found in fuel and beverages, as for example :—

Petrol	...	5d. a gallon.	Gin	... ...	2/6 a bottle
Coal	...	12/- to 15/- a ton	Whiskey ...	...	3/- a bottle
Candles	... ...	3d. a lb.	Ale	... ...	1/- a gallon
Firewood	...	½d. a bundle	Stout	... ...	2½d. a bottle

But almost equally great are the changes in furniture and household accessories ; both Jeffreys and Neudeggs of Northampton offered to furnish a house for £15, and a cottage for £6. Both offered discounts of 1/- in the £ for cash. Individual items of furniture were advertised as follows :—

Dining Room or Drawing Room Suites covered in leather	£3	3s. od.
Bedroom suites, various designs	£4	18s. 6d.
Brass Bedsteads		12s. 6d.
Blankets		10s. 11d.

From quite another source we have an interesting check on prices at the time. When Mr. and Mrs. Holloway were married in 1900 the bride kept a very careful account of all that she spent on her trousseau, and fifty-one years later, on Mr. Holloway's death the list came to light again.[1] In it were the following items :—

8 towels for bedroom	4/-
2 white quilts	19/5
1 pair long curtains	5/6
10 yards flannelette	4/-
3 nightdresses and 3 chemises and 1 bodice	18/3½
1 pr. blankets, best	17/11
1 pr. ditto	12/9
6 yds. calico for pillow cases at 3d. per yard	1/6
6 yds. white twill sheeting	7/3
2 under vests	3/1

[1] Mr. Holloway died at his residence at 183, Church Street, Wolverton in January 1951. I am indebted to the family and to Mr. Swain of Wolverton for permission to reproduce items from this list.

FLOODS AT STONY STRATFORD

In heavy rains there used to be a lake three miles long and about half a mile broad between Passenham and Cosgrove, and the flood water would come swirling into the High Street, Stony Stratford. Mr. Warr, the coal merchant, whose house is shown in the right, would convey passengers across the floods to Old Stratford for a penny a head.

Photographs lent by Miss MaGuire

SPRINGTIME IN 1902

High Street, Stony Stratford before the advent of motor traffic, when the quiet serenity of the town was only disturbed by dogs and babies. The old Chancel of St. Giles Church (demolished in 1927) can be seen on the right. Note the tram lines.

THE EARLIEST PHOTOGRAPH OF COSGROVE

A charming group showing the Warren family outside their house near the Brewery which Mr. Warren built in 1858. See p. 36.

PASSENHAM MILL

was in regular use up to about 1920. The chain in the foreground marks the way of the old ford still used up to that period. See p. 38.

1 table cloth	...	...	...	...	5/11
1 apron at	...	...	...	...	1/0¾
2 aprons at 1/11		...	...	...	3/10
4 yds. towelling at 4¾d. yd.		...	...	1/7

and so on. Looking down the young lady's list, which was, as far as a mere man can judge, very complete for the average type of house in this area, it is interesting to note that it totals £11 0s. 1¼d. The farthing was still a power in those days and most drapers' prices seemed to be " something and 11¾d.".

It is difficult to make a proper comparison between the standard of living then and now, since fashions and requirements have changed so much, but if we take the average wage then as being abouts 25s. a week, wages have increased six times as much in the past forty-five years.[1] On the other hand, clothing, coal and petrol have gone up by eight times as much, alcoholic beverages and furniture by about ten times as much, and food by about four times as much. And of course taxation on the working man has gone up by leaps and bounds since the first world war.

It would appear as if the average working man of the 1900's was better off than his son to-day, but other factors again have to be taken into consideration. Families then were larger, and children have large appetites and are heavy on clothing and boots ; also much more per family (comparatively to the value of money) was then spent both in intoxicating liquors and on the favoured Church. Another point is that on the railways there were usually four or five weeks at least during the year when the men were on " short time ", which meant that they lost about eight hours work and pay each week. But taking everything by and large, I think it is true to say that the temperate married man with the small family, or the temperate single man, was better off in 1906 than he is to-day, whereas the man with the large family (and by this I mean four or more children), the widows, women workers, and the elderly, are better off to-day, mainly due to the social legislation which

[1] The Board of Trade " Enquiry into the Earnings of Hours of Labour " for the years 1906 and 1907 showed that in those years the average wage of a railway worker was 25s. 10d., and that of the agricultural labourers varied from 12s. to 20s. 9d. Women workers in the printing industry earned about 12s. 4d. a week. Men in the engineering trades earned an average of 33s. 11d. per week, and the men in the printing trades 27s. 8d. per week.

began in 1908 and was continuously improved during the 1920's and 1930's.

Of course the ideal would be if we could have to-day's wages with the prices of the 1900's, but who knows if we might not have been somewhere near that but for the excessive drain on our resources of two world wars !

FOOD.

Whilst on the subject of food it may be mentioned that the housewife of the 1900's could never fall back on tinned goods, for the only tinned commodity available locally was corned beef, but this was in peculiarly bad odour owing to the scandals which then made the quality of such products very dubious. Indeed, such was the public awareness of what might or might not be " canned ", that one of the most popular get-ups at the local cycle carnival was a man surrounded with tins of beef, and a dead cat, and bearing the legend " We eat what we can, and we can what we cannot ".

There were, however, other household stand-bys, such as collared head, brawn, and sometimes a good ham. At this period the first shipments of chilled meat were coming in from the Argentine and New Zealand, a move that was met with the greatest opposition from the butchers who sold locally produced meat, and who challengingly exhibited placards with the legend " No foreign meat sold here ". Gradually, however, the cheapness of the chilled meat won it a market, and British agriculture entered upon one of its worst times.

There were other commodities in the food line which have now almost disappeared, such as the dripping with a deep jelly at the bottom that came, and indeed only could come, from the cooking of large joints. Faggots, made of liver and fry, with sage and onions were a favourite dish. Lard and suet could be bought freely, and were used freely. One of the interesting little points of the time was that men in Wolverton Works carried their lunches in little wicker baskets which would strap nicely on to the back of a bicycle. Alternatively, many had hot dinners taken to them by children who collected several from various houses at a time, and pushed the little trucks to the Works.

Other things which have disappeared were the pie-man and the muffin-man, with their bells and sonorous cries. The mention of the old street cries reminds one that lavender sellers also came around with their curious wailing song. Lavender seemed to be universally used for keeping chests of drawers sweet and fresh.

From food to tobacco is perhaps not such a long cry, and by the 1900's smoking had at last become tolerated to a moderate degree. Tobacco was cheap then, cigarettes were 2½d. for ten, whilst the cheaper brands of tobacco, such as " White Lily " was 3d. an ounce. Boys bravely smoked a rum kind of cigarette called " Jolly Jacks " which were 6 for a halfpenny.

Nearly all these various brands of cigarettes were now including " fag-cards " in their cartons, and the craze for collecting these beautifully printed pieces of pasteboard swept through every school.

LOCAL SHOPS

The advertisements of the *Wolverton Express* not unnaturally carry advertisements praising the wares of local tradesmen. Oldest of all these was the Chemist still known as " Cox and Robinson ", founded in 1760, and which still has one of the most fascinating shop fronts and interior fittings of any chemist's shop in the Midlands. The shop front dates from about 1840, but the shop-fittings are probably a century earlier, and include drug runs, and curved scalloped bottle runs, decorated with inscriptions in gold. Among the firm's heirlooms, then as now, is a delightful jar labelled " V. Diapomp . . .1679 ", old syrup jars, mortars and pestles, an ancient retort, a microscope of the 1850's, and still older record books, in one of which is the following quaint recipe for sheep ointment :—

Argentum	6 lb.
Rosin	9 lb.
Hyd. bichloride ...	
Bals. sulphur aa. ...	3 oz.
Adeps coml.	27 lb.

In the early 1900's Cox and Robinson was distinctly the ideal type of family pharmacy, for in addition to the usual work of chemists, they sold vinegar, soda water, tea, tobacco, and cigars. With very few exceptions every medicine sold was made up on the premises and some of the upper back rooms still contain packets of rare ingredients which were then used daily in the art of dispensing.

There were several other firms which could even in 1900 boast half a century of service to the people of Stony Stratford.

Odell's, the ironmongers, at 60-62 High Street, had been going since 1865, and were still causing trouble to the authorities and to pedestrians by their luxuriant display of pots and pans along the pavement. Canvin's, the butchers, dated from the 1860's, and were always remarkable for their rivalry with Higgs, the butcher, as to who could put up the best show of sucking pigs, prize beasts and so on for Christmas.

At Wolverton probably the oldest retail traders or craftsmen were Eadys, the butchers, Sigwart's, the jewellers, and Gurney's, the stone masons, all of whom have now been going for nearly a century. But at Newport there were still older retailers, for Lawman's, bakers and confectioners, were established in 1828, and the family did not relinquish the business until some years after the only surviving son was killed in the Second World War.

Shops and public houses were then open for long hours, for it was then the popular idea that a public house should always be open for the refreshment of travellers, and shops of course took their trade as they found it. It was not unusual then for most boys to become errand boys at the age of 13 or 14, and sometimes earlier for the part time work of delivering the morning's papers. The usual rate of pay for the full week's work of an errand boy was five shillings, which was the rate I started at, but my job was light compared with that of a schoolfriend of mine, Selby Davey, who at 13 became errand boy to a newsagent. His day started at 6.30 a.m. when he pushed a truck up to Wolverton and picked up the morning papers off the London train. Back to Stratford with the truck, he would then make the town deliveries on foot, and when this was finished go off to breakfast. After breakfast he would cycle (bike, is the proper word, for cycling has the element of a pastime in it, whereas this was pushing work in all weathers) to Cosgrove, Passenham, Deanshanger, Thornton, Wicken Park, Wicken, Starsmores, the Folly, and back to Stony Stratford. After a midday meal, he would go up to Wolverton Station again to fetch 12 copies of the *Northampton Echo*, deliver these, and his day was done. 30 miles a day for 5s. a week !

Mr. Selby Davey, then went into the Works, and after two successful efforts at running successively a milk round, and a fried fish shop on his own, both of which he sold well, is now enjoying a robust employment at Swindon.

" THE WOLVERTON EXPRESS "

Meanwhile, in 1901, Wolverton could claim for the first time that it had a newspaper of its own. Early that year a young man named Henry Ernest Bannard, who had served his apprenticeship as a printer, and had ambitions both as a historian and as a poet, decided to visit some relatives at Stony Stratford with the idea of starting a local paper at Towcester. He arrived at Wolverton Station, walked down to the Market, and stood watching in surprise the hundreds and hundreds of men as they teemed out of Wolverton Works. He found that Wolverton had no paper of its own, and decided that it ought to have.

Why not ? According to the Census figures Wolverton (which then included Old Wolverton and Wolverton St. Mary) had a population of just over 5,000 ; Stony Stratford just over 2,000, Stantonbury (or New Bradwell) nearly 4,000, and the adjacent villages brought up the total to over 14,000. He shrewdly calculated that if only every household in Wolverton and its immediate vicinity could be persuaded to buy a copy of a weekly paper there would be a circulation of about 2,000, and that would certainly be a paying proposition.

But there were arguments on the other side. There was the long established *Bucks Standard*, published at Newport Pagnell, which had been going since January 1859, and, under the fine editorship of Mr. Line,was still much appreciated in Wolverton ; here was a powerful and well-established rival. Then again, nobody had ever been able to run a successful weekly paper either from Stony Stratford or from Wolverton. Away back in 1854, Mr. Nixon, a printer living in the High Street, Stony Stratford, had produced the first local paper with the generous title of *The Cottage Newspaper and the Stony Stratford and Wolverton Station General Advertiser*, which struggled on for a decade, and died with him. A few years after his death another enterprising Stony Stratford High Street man, Alfred Walford, produced *The North Bucks Advertiser*, which had begun publication about 1870 and was still tottering along, under Mr. G. P. Eardley's editorship. In the meantime there had been the short-lived *Newport Pagnell Gazette, Wolverton Times and Olney Free Press*, established in 1867, but which had ceased publication within a few years.

Mr. Bannard, however, was not daunted by the rivalry either of the Newport Pagnell *Bucks Standard*, or by the Stony Stratford *North Bucks Advertiser*, and on Friday, April 17th, 1901, the first number of the *Wolverton Express* appeared.

So it was that the *Wolverton Express* came into being. Its first number consisted of four large pages (double the present sized page), and contained a local directory, the railway time table, and a fine article on " The Problem of the Aged Poor ". It was printed (as now) by the Bedford Publishing Company, and sold at 1d. Unfortunately no copies of the first two or three numbers appear to be available locally, and the only known copies are in the British Museum, but after this period there is a practically complete series of the paper still to be seen at the offices of the Wolverton Express.

Within a few months it was doubled in size, but four or five pages of the new paper had little or nothing to say about Wolverton and district, and for years afterwards half of the paper was taken up by syndicated news from all over the world, special columns devoted to Science Notes, Facts and Fancies, Hints for the Home, Garden Work, Words of Wisdom, Something for the Young, Yankee Humour, Bits from Books, The World of Women, and Business Abroad. In every issue there was also a serial story, usually from the pen of one of the most distinguished writers of the period, and from time to time there were special articles by authors of the quality of Mark Twain and Justin MacCarthy. The editorial quality of the paper was astonishing, and indeed of a quality as high as that of many of our great national dailies or the best of the Sunday papers of to-day. World news was reported in the grand manner, and local news with accurate objectivity.

The advertisement columns were not less interesting, for in addition to advertisements from local grocers, wine merchants, coal merchants, and so on, there were advertisements of a national and sometimes international nature. The Cunard Company, for instance, regularly advertised their shipping facilities, and there were other appeals to " Winter in Algeria " (which must surely have appealed dryly to the average railway worker of the time), or "Visit Royal Bad Oeynhausen, Germany, Summer and Winter Health Resort ", whilst a French firm advertised half-a-dozen bottles of Champagne for 67s. But let us leave the advertisements for a moment, and consider just what items were considered at this period to be of local interest.

THE WATER CART

In the days before the tarring of the roads, the dust was laid by a sprinkling from the local Council's water cart. Seated on the box is Mr. Ratley, horseman to the Council for many years. In the background is Church St. On the right may be seen the local cobbler, Mr. Dick Jennings, who lived to be 96. See p. 49.

GENERAL BOOTH DRIVES THROUGH IN A MOTOR CAR IN 1905

On July 15th, 1905 General Booth of the Salvation Army and his staff drove through Stony Stratford with a fleet of three motor cars. In those days there was no Highway Code, and the traffic was all over the place. The portly gentleman in shirtsleeves on the right is Mr. A. E. Pinfold, a local publican. The house on the extreme left (now belonging to Mr. Canvin) is built on the site of the old Angel Inn, which flourished about the time of the Civil War, and was then the first or last house in Stony Stratford.

Photograph lent by Tickford, Ltd.

MR. WALTER CARLILE'S CAR 1904

One of the first cars made by Messrs. Salmons and Sons, Ltd., of Newport Pagnell, was a Daimler Phaeton built for Mr. (later Sir) Walter Carlile in 1904. Mr. Carlile was the first Member of Parliament to travel to the House of Commons in a motor car. Note the tiller steering, gig candle lamps, solid tyres, wooden spokes, and chain drive. See p. 47. In the background is a portion of Sir Walter's house at Gayhurst, which was the scene of the " kill " described on page 105.

Then, as now, considerable space was given to the activities of the local authorities, and reports of the " Stony Stratford and Wolverton R.D.C. " figure prominently, as do the reports of the various local parish councils.

The local Volunteers took nearly a column in every issue, whilst in the camping season nearly half a page would be devoted to a description of their activities. Sermons too, would sometimes be printed at length, and bazaars, fetes, processions, etc., reported almost minutely. Sporting news varied, sometimes there would be whole columns of it, and sometimes a mere paragraph. Oddly enough, although there were attempts to create a " Births, Marriages and Deaths " column people seemed to be reluctant to publicise their family events.

For two years Mr. Bannard continued as Editor and then gave way to Mr. A. E. Jones, in May 1903. Mr. A. E. Jones brought a very solid business mind to the service of the paper, and gradually it flourished.

Shortly after his retirement from Wolverton, Mr. Bannard published his *School History of Berkshire*, but never lost touch with the *Wolverton Express*. As early as January 1907 we find him advocating in the columns that the County Council should run buses for school children and the general public. One of his very last contributions to the *Express* was his review in 1948 of *The History of Stony Stratford* which he did in a most kindly and generous way.

Illustrations were very few for years. Advertisements were, however, often illustrated, and the brass beds, upright pianos, perambulators, and so on, form the few illustrations in most issues. The fashion column was always illustrated by one or two sketches of the latest modes, and very amusing most of them are to modern eyes.

Meanwhile in January 1905 the *Wolverton Express* took over the *Stony Stratford Times* which had waged a losing struggle against its larger rival for several years. One result of the merger was to strengthen greatly the Stony Stratford side of the news in the *Express*, for the *Express* now took on to its staff Mr. George Barlow, and it is from this time onwards that we find the news from the Stony Stratford area as competently reported as any, and indeed often at greater length than the Wolverton news.

It is, as I have said in the Preface, mainly from the *Wolverton Express* that I have taken the background material for this book. It was a fascinating experience, and I am most grateful to the present Editor, Mr. A. J. Emerton, not only for the privilege, but also for the joy of absorbing some of the hopes and aspirations, some of the joys and struggles of an age which seems infinitely distant from us all now.

CHAPTER III

The Villages

AGRICULTURE

Then, as now, once away from the towns of Wolverton and Stony Stratford, and from the village of Deanshanger, the greater part of the local population depended upon agriculture for its livelihood. The Vale of Aylesbury had long been famed for the excellence of its agricultural produce, and it still held that high reputation. Cattle, sheep, pigs and horses from this neighbourhood had a grand renown, and the herds or flocks in the Argentine or other South American countries were often strengthened and improved by the import of Buckinghamshire stock.

The cattle were mostly sold at the local markets, and Stony Stratford, Winslow, Buckingham, Newport Pagnell, and so on all had thriving markets of considerable importance. But in addition to these there was the Leighton Buzzard wool fair, where no less than 15,000 fleeces were sold annually, and the Winslow Sheep Fair, where close on 2,000 sheep could be seen penned at a single time.

Many of our agricultural villages in 1900 were very much the same as they had been in 1800, and indeed in 1700. Three in particular do not seem to have changed much even to-day, Cosgrove, Passenham and Wicken.

COSGROVE

But early in the 1800's Cosgrove had had a great upset. For centuries it had been a " dead-end " village. Once into Cosgrove there was no way out, for it was bounded on three sides by the Rivers Ouse and Tove, and there were no bridges nearer than the Castlethorpe bridge to the north, or the Stratford bridge to the south-west. In 1805, however, this isolation was broken by the coming of the Canal, and Cosgrove found itself not only the junction of the main London and Birmingham route and the Buckingham arm, but also an important distributing centre, and the Canal Wharf at Cosgrove became for 30 years one of the busiest spots in the locality. But the coming of the railway in 1838 thrust Cosgrove back again into its somnolence, though it still continued to be a fairly busy barge centre until the coming of road transport.

One curious feature about the Buckingham arm was that it froze more quickly and solidly than either the River Ouse or the main canal. The fact was not only noted by skaters from miles around, but also by the owner of Cosgrove Hall, who, in some date round about 1820 built an "ice house" half-way between the canal and the Hall. This ice house was constructed rather like a stone windmill, with very thick walls, but whereas the windmill was entirely above ground, the ice house had its greater part below the level of the surrounding field. Into this ice house, every winter from 1820 to the 1900's ice cut from the canal would be stored, packed around with straw, and by this method it kept until the following spring and summer, when it would be sold to local fishmongers, butchers and others in the days before refrigeration was possible. The building still stands, though naturally not in its former condition, and is, I think the only ice house now remaining in Buckinghamshire, and one of the very few left in all England.

Not very far from the ice house was the Jaycock, a short arm of water jutting out from the canal where barges and boats of all kinds could be repaired or repainted.

Whilst on the subject of Cosgrove it is worth mentioning that the village boasts of one of the genuine "Holy Wells" safe-guarded by Act of Parliament. In a field just behind the old National School there is now to be seen a circular iron fence around a ruddy looking natural spring. This was the celebrated St. Vincent's Well, or Finches Well, a pure chalybeate spring of great healing value. When the Parish of Cosgrove was enclosed in 1767 there was a special clause in the Award saying that St. Vincent's Well should belong to the people of Cosgrove for ever, and that there should always be free access to it by a footpath from the public road. The water of this well has a very high iron content, and during the 1900's it was extensively used for the bathing of eyes, and was of particular value in conjunctivitis. Possibly it may have been "something in the water" that led Mr. Warren to build a brewery here in 1858. Mr. Warren and his family, with the brewery in the background, may be seen in one of our illustrations. The brewery continued to function for over half a century but under different ownership, whilst the descendants of Mr. Warren, and their relatives by marriage, the Plumbs, centred on Stony Stratford.

MILLS AND FLOODS

One of the lesser industries of the area at this period was the local milling. To-day as we survey the whole stretch of the River Ouse from Buckingham to Newport there is not a single mill working away at its traditional job of milling corn, but in 1901, and indeed for many years afterwards, every mill along this stretch of the river was busy, and the local miller was a man of importance. The two nearest mills were of course Old Wolverton Mill (locally known as Wood's or Norman's after the miller of the time) and the Stony Stratford Mill of which Mr. James Rogers was the respected and redoubtable owner. Like many other local millers, Mr. Rogers was also a farmer, and an extremely successful one. In addition to this he was unquestionably one of the best churchwardens any parish has ever had. First at Thornton, and then at Stony Stratford St. Giles, he held that office for 52 years, from 1876 to 1917.

Both at the Wolverton and the Stony Stratford Mill it was no infrequent sight to see the great wains rather like the film edition of a prairie schooner, pulled by two and sometimes four horses, coming to or from the mills. The mills not only ground the corn of the local farmers, but also sold flour direct to the public at 2d. for a 2 lb. bag.

The mills naturally depended upon water power, and it was the aim of every miller along the Ouse to keep his head of water just right, and there was a considerable art in the opening or shutting of sluice gates just at the right times. Near the sluice gates were nearly always to be found eel traps, brick sided holes about five feet deep, where, for some reason or other, eels would congregate and get caught by the dozen.

Although the millers were extremely interested in the level of the river, there was no general plan for the drainage of the locality. Throughout its length the river was rushy (a relic of the days when mats were made from them at the Stony Stratford mat factory on the Market Square, or at Newport Pagnell) and extremely weedy. Consequently when there were heavy rains, and it rained just as much in the 1900's as now, floods were frequent and vast. Scarcely a year went by without the floods coming over the High Street at Stony Stratford, and from Old Wolverton to Passenham there would be a great lake three miles long of swirling waters. In really bad seasons the floods at Stony Stratford would come up as high as the Cock Hotel, as they did in November 1894. It was not only in the winter season that these floods occurred, for in the June of 1903 there was the highest summer flood ever known. From the bridge to St. Oswald's House and from Passenham to Cosgrove was a solid expanse of water. One of the odd effects of this flood was that the sewerage system failed completely, and banks of foul smelling refuse piled up both by the Stony Stratford and the Old Wolverton Mills. The state of the local roads and lanes after such a visitation can well be imagined.

There was an administrative body known as the Ouse Drainage Board which was supposed to get farmers to clear out the river near their lands, but it had no powers adequate to the situation, and it was not until 1929, when it was replaced by the Ouse Catchment Board, that real efforts were made to keep the river clean and clear from obstructions.

These weedy rivers proved, however, a blessing to local anglers, for fresh water fish abounded. There was little water pollution then, and many stories are told of giant pike, perch, and other fishes which were caught. In addition to the rivers, the canal was also a popular venue for the followers of Isaac Walton, and fishing rights were jealously guarded by the local angling societies.

Both Passenham Mill and Bradwell Mill were reputed to be haunted. At Passenham the spectral figure of Nancy Lee, who drowned herself in the Mill Race was still supposed to be seen, whilst at Bradwell, Browne Willis in his Antiquities of Bucks mentions a tradition that the Mill was haunted. About 1685 the daughter of the miller, a very pretty girl, was sought in marriage by two youths, one of them killed the other in a fit of jealousy. He was gibbetted for his crime, and soon after the girl was found dead in one of the upper rooms of the mill.

PASSENHAM

One of the oddest features of our local lore is that of all the villages around Stony Stratford and Wolverton, Passenham is the one that gives rise to most of the ghost stories. It may of course be due to the comparative loneliness of the hamlet, the prevalence of owls in the neighbourhood, or the effect of the mist on humid evenings which rises from the several arms into which the River Ouse divides itself at this point. But it may well be due to a thousand year old cause, as a result of which skeletons are discovered from time to time in the oddest spots. In 1874, when the Rector was having a new floor put into his dining room, several skeletons were discovered only a few inches below the surface. Again, in 1916, when a great gale blew down several trees on the Stony Stratford end of the Passenham Lane, two skeletons were found embedded in the roots of one. More recently, in July 1947, workmen laying a drain only a few feet in front of the Rectory front door came upon three skeletons, again only a few inches below the surface of the ground. I was fortunate in getting the help of Dr. W. A. Swinton of the British Museum in elucidating the problems thus presented, and on July 25th, 1947, I published an article in the *Wolverton Express* of which the following is an extract :—

The skulls were all apparently those of young men in the prime of life, for the teeth were in excellent condition, not a sign of dental decay, though the molars seemed to be ground down somewhat more than a modern diet of soft foods would warrant. The thigh-bones were about 18 inches long, showing that these young men must have been nearly 5 ft. 9 in. tall. Four of the bodies were buried with the heads to the west and feet to the east, whilst the fifth was head to the east. Most of them had arms stretched alongside the bodies.

Now what are we to make of this ? In the first place, I think it will be agreed that no interments would have been made in front of the Rectory, and, indeed, close to its best rooms, once the Rectory had been built, so that the burials must be at least earlier than 1600 A.D. But for 400 years before this there had been a church and parson at Passenham, the earliest Rectors being William de Cirencester and Hugh de London, who both flourished about 1180 A.D. Once a church and churchyard are established, people like to be buried as near the church as possible, indeed burial outside the churchyard was the sign of a suicide or a felon. Consequently, it is possible that these burials took place before the first Rector took up his dwelling in the parish, i.e., before 1170 A.D.

We have already seen that most of the bodies were buried facing the east—a sign of Christian burial, and since this part of England was pagan up to about 650 A.D. we can fairly assume that they must have been buried after that date.

Our next question is, what happened in Passenham between the years 650 and 1170 A.D. that would lead to scores of burials over a fairly wide area ? Yes, scores of burials, for only a few years ago, Mr. A. Roberts, of Deanshanger, was one of a group which uncovered human bones in the old Tithe Barn, which dates from about 1500 A.D., and there is also on record the fact that other bones were discovered when a great elm tree, at least 400 years old, blew down during the course of a great storm.

As far as we can gather, during the whole of this period 650—1170 A.D. Passenham was little more than a small village, for, in the Domesday record, half the Manor was waste land, there was a wood " a mile square ", and only about twelve carucates of arable land (a carucate being as much land as could be cultivated by a man with a team of oxen in one year), and 30 acres of meadow land. But the Mill was already there, worth 13s. 4d. yearly, and probably a dozen other dwellings. The Manor then belonged to the King, and is spelt either " Bassonha" or " Passeha ".

A century or more earlier than this, Passenham had been the scene of great activity. The history books tell us that in 866 A.D. England was invaded by the Danes, and that within ten years they had occupied the whole of East Anglia, Mercia (which included Passenham), and even parts of Wessex. Alfred the Great put a heroic resistance to their further advance, and in 878 the Peace of Wedmore divided all England into two halves, the Danelagh and the English area, the boundary between them being the Thames, the Lea up to its source near Leighton Buzzard, then due north to Bedford, then westwards along the River Ouse to Stony Stratford, thence northwest along the Watling Street. Castlethorpe became a Danish camp, Buckingham an English (or Anglo-Saxon) camp.

From 907 onwards, Alfred the Great's second son, Edward the Elder, worked for the recovery and conquest of the Danelagh. Whilst Buckingham and Towcester were being fortified he pitched his camp at Passenham. The Anglo-Saxon Chronicle records that " In 921 A.D. the Danes, having attacked and injured Towcester, King Edward the Elder, having repulsed them, lay with his army at Passenham whilst Towcester was better secured against future irruptions by a stone wall ". About this time Northampton submitted, the Danes of that " borough " coming to Passenham to make their submission.

Where was this camp at Passenham? The great historian, Bridges, writing about 1700-20, conjectured that " the almost square entrenchment which is still remaining near the old ford, was probably raised on this occasion (by Edward the Elder) as a guard to that passage over the Ouse ". This square entrenchment of a mound and moat around it can still be seen running right across the cricket field near Shady Corner, the cricket pavilion standing on the highest point. A thousand years have naturally rounded off the original rampart and ditch, but I have no doubt, that this peculiar and striking feature on the ground owes its origin to our Anglo-Saxon forefathers. From this camp there were constant comings and goings to Towcester, and the track or road through Puxley, or Pochlesei, must have been in great use.

It is easy to realize that among the few thousand men which then made up an army, there must have been some wounded or sick, and that some of these died and were buried willy-nilly where convenient. As we have said, the skeletons that have come to light were those apparently of young men—so it would appear that the many bones which have come to light were those of some of our Anglo-Saxon ancestors who held the camp at Passenham a thousand years ago. We cannot, however, be absolutely certain about this, for neither brooch nor pin, neither weapon nor tool, has been found with the bodies.

We can, however, be certain that at least four times in the past 100 years, skeletons have been found in the oddest spots at Passenham, and it may be that these gave rise to various conjectures and suppositions that resulted in " ghost stories ".

But this would not explain the alleged " ghost " of Sir Robert Bannister or Bannestre. In 1620 this jovial squire bought the Passenham estate from the King. In the following years he not only beautified the church, and rebuilt the Manor, but also added a new wing to the large Tithe Barn, the first part of which had been erected in the time of Henry VIII. One of the door-ways of the new wing bears the date 1626, so that we may assume that this was the date of its erection.

Sir Robert Bannestre was apparently no less active in death than in life if we are to believe local legends that were current during the 18th and even 19th centuries. In a very rare pamphlet, entitled " The History of Passenham ", published by William Nixon, Printer and Stationer, of Stony Stratford, in

1856 there occurs this footnote : " The following much abridged ghost story passes current yet in the hamlet of Denshanger. Sir Robert Bannestre, once an occupier of the Mill at Passenham, after his decease, so often revisited that neighbourhood, that six men, eminent for piety, were required to lay his spirit, once and for ever afterwards, in the bottom of the mill dam ".

Thus the story of " Bobby Bannestre's Ghost " was first published in 1856.

Leaving the subject of ghosts we may just glance at the history of Passenham after the death of the last of the Bannestres, for it then descended to the Maynards. After Viscount Maynard's death in 1843 the Manor descended to his son, the Hon. Charles Henry Maynard, who in 1860 married Blanche Adeline Fitzroy. Their eldest daughter was Frances Evelyn, Countess of Warwick, who came into the family estates in 1865. These included a dozen Manors and half a dozen Rectories in Essex, and the entire Manor of Passenham, which then contained about 840 acres, and the Advowson of the Rectory. It was this Countess of Warwick who was one of the great friends of King Edward VII when he was Prince of Wales, and she was one of those who helped to make the gay court scenes of the latter part of the 19th century. She spent, of course, far more time in London than at Passenham, and the decision in 1911 to sell the whole of the Passenham Estate was not unexpected. At this sale in 1911 the Lands of the Manor, were much as they had been since the Enclosure Award of 1772, and probably for several centuries earlier. They included practically all the land between Deanshanger, Old Stratford, and Passenham, including Northfields Farm, Old Stratford Farm (now known as Home Farm), as well as the whole of Puxley Grange Farm totalling 244 acres. The " Particulars of the Sale " gives us the old names of all the various fields in Passenham, including not only the familiar ones of " Windmill Field ", " Robins Ley ", " Shoulder of Mutton ", " Dry Hills ", and so on, but less familiar ones such as " Nell Perry's Ground " and " The Breaks " at Passenham and " The Assarts " at Puxley.

WHITTLEWOOD FOREST

Right up to the middle of the 19th century the four great landowners in the Deanshanger—Passenham area were the Lord of the Manor of Passenham, Lord Penrhyn, the Duke of Grafton and the King who through the Commissioners of Crown Lands still owned the greater part of Whittlewood Forest. This forest, as is recorded in Domesday, extended right down to Old Stratford, and stretched as far west as Akeley, and as late as 1791 the whole area between Old Stratford, Deanshanger, Wickenhurst, and Puxley was still dense forest. But early in the 19th century the area between Puxley and the Watling Street, including Bears Watering Copse and Eustilus Copse, was cleared. In 1853 the remaining part between Puxley and Old Stratford was cleared. Sallow Copse, Pond Riding Copse, and Cole Copse resounded to the lumberman's axe, and by 1860 the area had been turned over to farming. At the same time the forest between Puxley and Wicken, including Hanger Walk, Wakefield Walk, and Sholbrook Walk, was cleared. The last remaining part of Whittlewood Forest in the Passenham—Deanshanger parish is now the spinney near Shrob Lodge. Further north, of course, there are still extensive parts of the forest left between Whittlebury and Potterspury.

PROPERTY

One of the interesting features of the period of which we write is that whilst prices generally, and wages, and house property were gently rising, the value of land was going down. In those days a cottage in a village could be bought for £30, but naturally this would have no modern amenities and would in all probability be a thatched picture with two rooms up and two down. The better type of cottage, as for example in King Street, Stony Stratford, was now, in 1905, being sold for £100, and was let for 5s. per week. A slightly better type of house in Russell Street or Wolverton Road, let at 6s. per week, and sold for £160. The average type of house in Wolverton was now being sold for £150 to £200.

Larger houses were not often in the market, but it is interesting to record that York House, London Road, sold for £810 in 1905, and No. 48 High Street, then a lovely Queen Anne House with Elizabethan stables was sold for £550. The ensuing years saw slight increases in these prices, but after the 1914-18 war prices took a great jump, and in fact almost doubled.

It was far different with land. For many years British agriculture had been under a cloud, and indeed was to remain under a cloud until the first world war, when U-boat warfare made people realise how valuable an asset our agriculture was, but at the time of which we are writing the challenge of cheap American and Argentine wheat and meat, with the newer methods of chilling and freezing meat, all reduced the returns to the English farmer, an ever growing number of whom found their way to the bankruptcy courts. Typical of the loss of the value of land under these circumstances can be gathered from the story of the Manor of Haversham. The entire parish is about 1,600 acres, and of this the slightly larger portion was from the earliest days attached to the Manor. In 1710 Lord Haversham sold the Manor to the Knightleys for £24,500. A century later William Greaves bought the Manor and 503 acres for £15,500 whilst the Mill and 360 acres were assigned to Roger Ratcliffe for £6,000. In 1903 Thomas Greaves sold the Manor to Henry Shaw for £12,500. In 1919 it was sold to Price Jones for £11,000, and in 1922 to Col. Edwin Pickwood for £7,000. On the Colonel's death in 1932 the Manor and 315 acres were sold for £3,150. Allowing for the fact that the acreage attached and the Manor had decreased over two centuries, the fall in the value of the Manor and land is astonishing.

On the other hand, land ripe for building purposes could command a respectable figure, and in the neighbourhood of Wolverton and Stony Stratford would fetch between £150 to £200 an acre.

CHAPTER IV

The Coming of the Motor Car

I SUPPOSE THAT the first motor car to have been seen in this locality must have been well before the death of Queen Victoria, since Stony Stratford is on one of the most important roads in the whole country, and both that town and Wolverton are on the principal road between Oxford and Cambridge, but there are actually few mentions of motor cars in the *Wolverton Express* until May 27th, 1904, and, as perhaps might have been expected, it is in Police Court News that motorists and their activities first appear. At that time the motorist and his car were violently disliked by most people living in rural areas : their contraptions were infernally noisy, and they always left a cloud of dust and oil vapour behind them. In those days roads were not macadamised or asphalted ; mostly there was a rolled gravel or chipped granite surface, untarred and untreated in any way, so that the passage of any vehicle, even a pony and trap, in fine weather inevitably raised a fine gritty cloud of dust. Ponies and traps of course went at a pace of only a few miles per hour, but the new Juggernauts could travel at a speed as high as forty to forty-five miles an hour, and once they got up to a speed of this kind they were very reluctant to use the brakes when passing through villages, and anyway the brakes were not very efficient. The Northamptonshire Police took steps to check these whirlwind progresses, and at Potterspury the minions of the law set up a speed trap complete with stop watches.

At the Stony Stratford Petty Sessions on Friday, May 20th, 1904 four motorists were summoned for travelling at speeds estimated to be 30 miles per hour through Potterspury. Three were fined £5 and costs, but the fourth, Percy Martin, of Coventry, was of a tougher disposition. Police Sergeant Norman, two Constables, and the Parish Constable gave evidence to the effect that Percy Martin had driven his car at the rate of a measured quarter of a mile in 25 seconds, which worked out at a speed of 30 to 40 miles per hour. Mr. Percy Martin contested this. He had come through the village at a speed of only 15 or

16 miles per hour, and " had sounded his horn all the way ". When he descended the hill " the power of his engine was thrown off ", and he was travelling only at about 8 miles per hour ; when challenged he pulled up within 50 or 60 yards. Two passengers of his gave corroborative evidence. The Bench took the view that there was a doubt as to whether the pace was dangerous to the public and dismissed the case.

A few weeks later there is recorded the first motor fatality in the district, when a small boy was killed at Shenley. This, as the paper said, " will cause many who have an inveterate hatred for motor cars to condemn the new method of travel more vehemently than ever. But motor cars are necessary evils now-a-days, and serious accidents from them are few and far between in this neighbourhood ". The motorist was completely exonerated, but the Coroner, Mr. E. T. Worley, in summing up, went on to say : " For my part, I wonder there are not more accidents, considering the legislature had allowed what are practically railway engines to run along the highway ".

Local hostility to motors and motorists was by no means assuaged by the behaviour of motorists themselves, some of whom behaved with a rudeness and even brutality which is inconceivable to-day. In July 1905, for instance, at 3 a.m. Police Constable Barrell was on duty at Deanshanger when he saw a motor car, " a tri-car with a wicker fore-carriage ", approaching the Green from the Buckingham Road. As the car had no lights the Constable held up his hand for the car to stop. The motorists yelled at him " Get out of the way or I'll run you over". Then the Constable was hit across the face and knocked over by the car, which went on without stopping. The Constable, seriously injured managed to crawl to his lodgings, leaving a trail of blood behind him. In spite of all enquiries, the culprits were never discovered.

In October 1906 another motorist, Mr. Borritt, of Hatton Court, near Castlethorpe, was involved in two accidents. In the first a young lady, Miss Dorothy Hall, daughter of a Stony Stratford tradesman, was knocked off her bicycle, and whilst she herself received " only a few bruises and a shock to her nervous system ", the cycle was smashed beyond recognition. The motorist drove on leaving the young lady to get home as best she could. In the same week the same motorist in the same area (Old Wolverton) was involved in another accident. A boy of 12, Harry Tooley, of Stony Stratford, (fortunately still alive) was pushing a truck down Old Wolverton Hill, when suddenly he heard a car coming behind him. The frightened lad let go of the truck and clambered into the hedge. The truck careered across the road only to be overtaken and smashed by the car. This time the motorist stopped, ran after the boy, and smacked his face! It was such incidents as these which were responsible for the real hatred of the new form of locomotion in this area for many years.

Nevertheless, it had its devotees who were equally enthusiastic for it. Probably the two earliest motorists in this neighbourhood were The Rev. G. M. Capell, of Passenham, and Mr. " Puffer " Atkinson, of Cosgrove. The Rev. Capell, who was Rector of Passenham for 44 years—from 1870 to 1914, was a charming man with a torpedo beard and an inventive mind. He had been responsible for many successful inventions, principally relating to extraction fans for mines, the prototypes of which were made up by Mr. Roberts, the Stratford blacksmith. As can be imagined the motor car received much attention from him, and his chuffing, tiller model, De Dion, was a joy to all. I believe that Mr. Atkinson's car was a Benz, improved locally by Mr. Hamilton, who subsequently set up an important garage at the Old Stratford cross roads. But whether homemade or not, all observers agreed that the cars were extremely noisy, and created dreadful clouds of dust whenever they came honk-honking along the highway. And joy was high when one or the other of these cars broke down, and faithful old Dobbin was hitched in front to tow it ingloriously home.

Mr. Hamilton soon had a rival in motor engineering, for Mr. Negus, of Stony Stratford, set up in 1902 the first garage in the town (now Messrs. R. J. Fleming), and was very happy to be able to sell petrol to all and sundry at the then ruling price of 5d. per gallon. It was Mr. Negus who first advertised " two 15 h.p. cars for hire "—and that was as late as November 1909.

Of all the local firms which helped on the new method of locomotion, none were perhaps more useful than the Salmons family at Newport Pagnell. Early in the 19th century Joseph Salmons took over the business of coach builder and harnessmaker at Tickford End, and very soon the name of Salmons acquired a fine local repute for the creation of first-class horse vehicles. It was here that the " Newport Pagnell Coach " was built, and some hundreds of gigs, broughams, bakers carts, and so on. The second Joseph Salmons carried on the tradition, and when he reached the age of 60, in 1896, he, and his sons, George and Lucas, decided to add the business of making bodies for the new motor cars to the older business.

The business throve, and when Joseph Salmons the second died in 1909, the firm of Salmons was known throughout Europe as makers of first-class motor bodies. The firm, shortly after the first world war, began to make its own car, the " N.P.", starting at a time when such young giants as William Morris (now Lord Nuffield) were already in the field. The " N.P." could never really compete with the Austin's or Morris's, and financially the firm found that difficulties were insuperable until it gave up the " N.P." car and settled down to the historic line of " Tickford " bodies.

Meanwhile, Newport had become very automobile minded, in great contrast to the towns of Wolverton, Stony Stratford, and Buckingham, where resentment against the new vehicle was slow to die.

This great change brought into fierce discussion the rights of users of the King's Highway. There were many who argued that the pedestrian had the first right to its use : their life was usually short. Others argued that the road was the preserve of vehicles, and that footpaths along the road side had been for centuries specially made and kept up for the use of pedestrians. Parliament and the judges wavered, and the nearest they ever came to a decision was that motorists were to be exonerated from all blame if a pedestrian ran across the road, and was knocked down, but that the motorists were to blame if they drove dangerously. From county to county there were different interpretations of what " driving to the public danger " meant, and even now the term is not really settled. In the meantime, the men and women and children of the 1900's were learning the first elements of road sense, to scutter to the path whenever the honk of a motor horn was heard.

THE ROADS

One of the curious features of this period was the shocking state of the roads. One would have thought with slow moving horse traffic, and very little motor traffic there would be so little wear and tear on the roads that once made good they would last for a decade or more. But the very opposite was the

Photograph lent by Mrs. Watts

OUT FOR THE DAY IN THE 1900'S

The ladies of the Conservative Association Branch at Wolverton set out for a jaunt in
a brake. Mrs. Tarry, the wife of the host of the Victoria Hotel is seeing them off. Small
boys naturally wanted to sit by the driver. See p. 51.

Photograph lent by Mr. F. S. Woollard

OUT FOR A DRIVE IN THE 1900'S

Most of the larger hotels had landaus or victorias for hire. Our photograph shows
Mrs. F. W. Woollard and some members of her family driving around Thornton. The
coachman is Mr. Hawkins, the story of whose death is told on p. 51.

DEANSHANGER CANAL WHARF

For nearly a century this wharf and that of Messrs. E. & H. Roberts, were the distributive centres for much that came into Deanshanger. The canal is now disused, and the wharf has become a garden.

Photographs by J. W. Smith

YARDLEY GOBION IN THE EARLY SUMMER OF 1902

The village pump, and the adjacent well were in constant use, whilst the miller's cart was on its weekly run from Stony Stratford to Northampton.

case, and even in the towns themselves the streets and roads were full of puddles and mud, and often very dangerous, whilst in summer the dust nuisance was abominable.

In May 1904, the Surveyor to the Stony Stratford and Wolverton District Council, published his fifth annual report, and in it there occurs this paragraph :—

Probably no road in the county has more mechanically propelled traffic than the Watling Street, and when, as in the case of the High Street at Stony Stratford, it becomes the main street of the town, with many business premises on either side, it becomes very necessary that every effort should be made to keep down the dust. At frequent intervals during the day motor cars can be seen passing, the course of each being marked by a cloud of dust, which hangs in the air for a considerable time afterwards, and in any normal season regular and plentiful sprinkling of the High Street will be necessary.

But dust was not the only trouble, there was also the mud. The pounded gravel of most roads, plus a liberal admixture of horse manure and clayey earth from local fields or paths, produced, whenever it rained, a swashy glutinous substance that made all progress dirty and difficult. And of course the potholes in the local streets produced puddles of uncertain depth. The local remedy for this at the time was the sludge cart, the whole idea of which was that the mud should be scraped or pushed into sloppy heaps and then shovelled into the large rectangular tank which formed the main part of the sludge cart. Complaints to local councils that the sludge cart had not been around were frequent, and they came not only from villages like Milton Keynes, where the mud was sometimes nine or ten inches deep, but also from most of the streets in Wolverton from time to time.

Quite early in the *Wolverton Express* we find complaints about the deplorable state of Creed Street and Ledsam Street, not a square yard of which, according to reports, was level. Time and time again the question was ventilated at the local Council, but the reply always made was that these were railway streets, and the local council was not responsible.

But this argument could not possibly apply to the Wolverton—Stratford road, and in 1906 we read that this was " simply a " disgrace. Not only is the mud up to one's neck, but the " whole of the left-hand side from Wolverton to Stratford is " dangerous to vehicular traffic, it is anything but level ".

It is small wonder that the great majority of houses up to this period still included as a regular fitting a foot-scraper near the front-door, and it was not until a decade later that roads and pavements received anything like satisfactory attention in this locality.

The solution to the problem of dust and mud was found at last in the comparatively simple process of tarring the roads. It was originally tried out at Stony Stratford in 1907, and was an undoubted success. In 1908 it was extended to the Wolverton Road, and to the Stratford Road at Wolverton. But even this solution had its opponents, for there were many who said, with some truth, that it made the roads slippery for horses (the final sanding only came in some years later), and there were others who said that at the cost of 1d. per square yard it was far too expensive.

The last reference we have to the clouds of dust that used to occur before tarring of the roads was adopted is in the *Wolverton Express* for August 1907, when a Wolverton resident complains bitterly that since the water cart is not used on Sundays the clouds of gritty dust raised by cars were an abominable nuisance.

It was about this time that two other developments came in which made the roads safer, the practice of shopkeepers installing gas lamps outside their shops, and the introduction of the incandescant gas mantle, which greatly improved the quality of the light. Stony Stratford High Street on a week-day night was now well lit from end to end, for the first time in history. Oddly enough, the public lamps were never lit on nights alleged to be moonlight.

But there was no lighting as yet in the villages, and often the only cheerful sign of human existence was the lamp-light streaming through the red blinds of the public houses.

The motors brought another great change. From the coming of the railway in 1838, towns like Stony Stratford along the main highways suffered a severe decline. In the early part of the 19th century Stratford had nearly thirty stage-coaches a day, to say nothing of private vehicles, the great majority of which stopped at the Cock, the Bull, or other of the noted Inns, but the railways killed all that, and with the new century there were left only the carriers to the villages, the dog-carts of the local gentry, and the occasional wagonette. The great Inns had become lowly pubs, but still catered for the annual political or regimental dinners in addition to their normal trade of selling what the brewers brewed.

But now traffic was beginning to flow back along the roads : oddly enough, however, the Inns made little attempt to cater for it. For the horse traffic, every inn had its stables, its ostler, its great supplies of oats and hay ; but few inns in the locality welcomed the new travellers by putting in petrol supplies, or engaging a mechanic to supplement the ostler. The new trade went to the new establishments rejoicing in the French name " Garage ", but the Inns of course still were glad to put motorists up for the night, though motorists were not particularly pleased to have to park their cars in stables or barns. The new garages flourished, and so brought an added prosperity to the towns along the highways.

How slow the local hotels were to welcome the motor trade is evident from the advertisements for a leading hotel in Stony Stratford as late as 1909, when motor traffic was becoming considerable. In that year the Bull Hotel advertised its :

BRAKES, WAGONETTES AND DOG CARTS
LANDAUS AND BROUGHAMS
HEARSE AND CARRIAGES

and underneath, in small type follows : " Every accommodation for motors and cyclists ".

Nearly all the inns and hotels kept some form of transport and a horse or two. The larger hotels, like the Cock and the Bull still had quite a selection, though nothing like what they had in the old coaching days. Still, they would mostly have a brougham, a landau or Victoria, a " fly " or cab, and a " gig " or dog-cart. The brougham and a pair of greys was the favourite for weddings, the Victoria or landau for a gentle drive on a sunny day, such as can be seen in another illustration ; the fly was used mainly for taking people and luggage to the railway station, whilst the gig or dog-cart seemed to be the favourite of commercial travellers to whom speed mattered. Over and apart from all these were the wagonettes, which seated four each side at the back, and the brake, six a side, and three at the front, which were largely used for " outings " by clubs and organisations from the football teams to the Women's branch of the local Conservative Association. We show an illustration of one of these leaving Church Street, Wolverton, for a drive to Woburn or Wakefield, great favourites for these outings.

It is interesting to recall that although the turnpikes, or toll-bars, had been abolished for about half a century, that on the Stony Stratford side of the bridge being abolished in 1857, the houses and posts were still in being, and it was one of these "pikes" that caused in December 1908 the death of the coachman seen in the illustration of the landau. He was Mr. William Hawkins, for many years coachman to Dr. Maguire, and subsequently ostler at the Bull Hotel. One night there came the call to go to Cosgrove with a fly, which, as older people may remember, had a high seat with a low surrounding rail in front of the cab itself. The fly reached the "Dog's Mouth", a local spring of great purity, nearby which was the old pike. The night was dark, and the feeble lamps of the fly did not help much. A wheel struck the pike, and Hawkins was thrown out head first and the fly passed over him. He died within a few hours.

One other experiment in public transport deserves to be mentioned. Somewhere around 1900 a few of the more progressive people in Newport Pagnell, including Mr. Charles Lawman, the confectioner, and Mr. Lucas Salmons, decided that the time was right for an up-to-date conveyance from Newport to Olney. Many years before, plans had been laid for a railway to run between those two towns, and the line of its proposed track through Bury Field can be seen in the "cutting" there to this day. In addition to this, special bridges were built alongside North Bridge and Sherington Bridge to carry the line; but the undertaking proved more expensive than was anticipated, and the work ceased without Olney ever seeing a train.

Undeterred by this history, our enterprising band bought a very remarkable vehicle, a two cylinder $4\frac{1}{2}$ h.p. motor bus. Unfortunately these were the very early days of motoring, and this particular vehicle had neither a reliable engine nor reliable brakes. To overcome the latter defect a "sprag" was fitted, a kind of iron spike, which, when the vehicle came to a stop on a hill, was let down by the conductor in the hope that it would dig into the road and so arrest the progress of the vehicle. Unfortunately the bus had a habit of "jumping the sprag" and proceeding regardless down hill backwards. As can be imagined ladies were not at all impressed by the device, and this, combined with the unreliability of the engine, caused the whole concern to be a complete financial loss.

The story illustrates one very important point. In those days anybody could start a bus service, or open a shop, or branch out in a hundred and one ways. The results were two-fold. Anyone who could give the public better service than before succeeded, and rich were the rewards to men of foresight who could produce a reliable service or article, but on the other hand, if the service or article were a failure, it was the individual, or group of individuals, who bore the entire loss.

One of the features of the transport of this period, which has now almost completely disappeared, was that of the local " carrier ". He was usually a very respectable person, owning a horse and van, who at regular intervals made a journey usually from a given public house, between two or more villages. At Stony Stratford, for example, there were in 1907 no less than six who thus served the town. The full list is as follows :—

Alderton	Mr. Jelly, from the Crown Inn on Fridays.
Castlethorpe and Hanslope	Mr. Eakins from the Crown Inn on Fridays.
Passenham Deanshanger Wicken and Buckingham	Mr. Mabbutt, Mondays and Thursdays.
Loughton	Mr. Jenkins, from the White Horse on Fridays.
Nash	Mr. Collier, from the Crown on Fridays.
Newport Pagnell	Mr. Mabbutt, on Fridays.
Northampton	Mr. Mabbutt, on Wednesdays and Saturdays.
Towcester	Mr. Mabbutt, on Tuesdays.
Whaddon	Mr. Masters, from the White Horse on Tuesdays and Fridays.

Mr. Robert Mabbutt who was a carrier in excelsis, had his own house in the High Street, and was, I think, the last of the great carriers who earned their living by carrying parcels, letters, and even small boys, from the market towns to the rural villages. Nothing was too much trouble for him, and whether his particular care was a barrel of oil, or a score of rose trees or a dog, he looked after it, and charged according to a reckoning of his own, which was very reasonable.

CHAPTER V.

Churches and Chapels

IT HAS ALREADY been mentioned that this area of the Buckinghamshire Ouse has few tourists and trippers, most travellers in these parts hurry through, whether on the arterial A.5 or on the British Railways, but however swift the transit, none can fail to notice one of the greatest features of this Midland scene, the ancient churches which fit so exquisitely into the landscape. Yet even amongst these there are few which attract the traveller from his path, for we have no Saxon crypt, as at Wing, or sheer Norman glory as at Stewkley. Several indeed can boast interesting Norman work, as at Stanton Low, Calverton, Bletchley, Hanslope, Whaddon and Shenley, but in the main most of our churches date from after 1300, and several from the 1800's.

Yet peaceful as the rural scene was around here in the 1900's, no one could claim that there existed between the churches and chapels the entire spirit of Christian brotherly love, for between these two great Christian divisions there was still a mutual suspicion and dislike which in these days of greater tolerance seems almost incredible.

Perhaps it all dates back to the Civil War, when the established Church supported Charles I, and the non-conformists to a man supported Cromwell; and both hated the Catholics. In these parts particularly there had been many persecutions in the name of Christianity, and indeed it was not until the Toleration Act of 1689 that the persecutions ceased. But this did not mean that friction ceased. At Stony Stratford, for example, there followed a two-century quarrel over the local charities, which the Church people held had been left for their benefit, whilst the non-conformists held that they had been left for the benefit of the town, and that all should be eligible. When the Parish Councils were established 1895 new fuel was added to these sectarian fires by the non-conformist demands for full enquiry as to how these charities had been carried out, and by the representatives of the Church of England telling them to mind their own business if they had any.

Thus, in 1900, the social and cultural gulf between Church and Chapel was deep and unbridgeable. Indeed it was only on occasions like the Diamond Jubilee, or the Coronation that the two could be found working together for the common good, for on lesser occasions, such as the opening of the almshouses, known as " The Retreat ", in 1893, the Church refused all invitations to be present.

These divisions were heightened by the politics of the day, for the Conservative ideas of educational development and the Liberal wish to Disestablish the Church of Wales, threw all non-conformists into the Liberal camp, whilst churchgoers were Conservative. This division of the nation into two camps was not lightly bridged. I remember an occasion in my own family which caused quite a comment. My father was Church of England, though as the Rev. Light remarked, his support was more like that of a buttress than that of a pillar, since he was mostly outside the Church. But my father had a great desire to know and see other religions. Early in the 1900's we once went to a Prayer Meeting in the Orphanage—in a great marquee in the grounds—and enjoyed the stirring hymns and friendly warmth of the occasion. Later that week there was a row— a mild one it is true—but nevertheless a row, for the Vicar came to remonstrate with my father against his " bad example ", and my father replied very sharply that we were all worshipping the one God.

This is a trivial incident, but it helps to show that during the 1900's the differences between Church and Chapel were acute, and indeed the difference did not even begin to evaporate until during and after the first World War.

There were equally acute differences within the Church of England itself, for during the last half century there had been gathering the struggle between " High " and " Low " Church.

The division had caused much controversy within the Church as can be imagined, and finally (though not so finally as it appeared) Parliament passed a Church Discipline Act in 1907 which was to produce great local excitement of which we shall write later.

Looking back over half a century, unquestionably one of the greatest changes is the decline of the churches. In the early years of this century England was still in the stuffy comfortableness of the Victorian era, and certainly as far as the rural areas were concerned Sunday was celebrated in the same way as had happened for centuries past. Almost everybody went to church sometime or other. Naturally the housewives with young families found this difficult, and there were undoubtedly many breadwinners who preferred to spend Sunday with the *News of the World* followed by a visit to the local ; but in popular estimation everybody who was " respectable " went to church, and we can gather what this meant in actual numbers when we read in the columns of the *Wolverton Express* that almost every church or chapel had an extension or some other improvement during this period.

The Church of England was very strongly entrenched, for in addition to the mother churches of Calverton and (Old) Wolverton, there were the elder daughters of St. Giles, Stony Stratford, and the relatively baby churches of St. James', Stantonbury, Wolverton St. George's, and Wolverton St. Mary's, all of which had been built during the 19th century.

It is invidious to single out any particular church to illustrate the point about local support at this period, and to mention all would prove far too long for this short book, so we must be content to take the Parish of Wolverton St. George's as a very good sample of what was then happening.

WOLVERTON ST. GEORGE'S

At this time the incumbent was the young and popular Reverend (later Canon) William Lee Harnett, M.A., who in 1896 had succeeded his equally popular father, the Rev. F. W. Harnett in that office. Canon Harnett's popularity extended well beyond church circles, for he was always ready to give papers before the local Literary and Scientific Societies, and showed no little grasp of scientific questions. In 1896 the work of adding wide transepts and a vestry was completed at a cost of £3,000, and at the same time the nave was re-seated in oak by the voluntary work of the congregation. A few years later an oak lobby was added to the west door, the chancel lengthened, and a clergy vestry erected, all of which cost £2,000. The Assistant Curate was then the Rev. W. Duncan Standfast. In 1906 a new organ was bought for £520, and a hydraulic blower added, a year later for £62. In 1908 the transepts were re-seated in oak, and in the same year the well designed Church Institute and Sunday Schools at the corner of Church Street and Creed Street, were opened. These had cost over £4,000. So that all in all, St. George the Martyr's had raised nearly

£10,000 (worth £50,000 to-day) in just over 10 years for Church purposes. It is only fair to add that in all these developments, as with most other developments in Wolverton and Bradwell, the London and North Western Railway[1] were generous donors, but this does not detract from the splendid effort that all Church workers in Wolverton had made to meet the requirements of the Parish.

The success of Wolverton in building its Church Institute led to an emulative attempt on the part of Stantonbury, which had a very extraordinary and long delayed result. In 1908 a fund known as the Stantonbury Church Institute Fund was started by a collection and organised events of the kind already described for Wolverton, and before long several hundreds of pounds were collected. But in the ensuing years some differences arose as to how it should be spent, meanwhile the money lay in the bank steadily accumulating interest. It stayed there during the first World War, and during the twenty years of peace that followed ; it stayed there during the second World War, and it was only in 1949 that the original Secretary (Mr. F. H. Tompkins) and one of the original Trustees (Mr. C. Wylie) and other surviving members of the first Committee took the decision with their newer colleagues that the money, now over £1,600, should be used to place a stained glass window in the Church, the remainder of the fund going to other churches in the town. But the Minister of Education refused to assent to such a proposition, and finally, in December 1950 it was decided, with the approval of the Minister of Education, to distribute it for the maintenance of buildings used by the churches for social and recreational purposes. St. James received approximately £1,000, the Methodist and Baptist churches £229 each, and the Salvation Army £150.

It is interesting to recall that when St. James was being built in 1858, £2,500 was subscribed by shareholders of the London and North Western Railway, whilst the pulpit bears the inscription : " The offering of the foremen and workmen in the Engine Factory, Wolverton ". The new parish had been formed in 1857 and the church consecrated in 1860.

In addition to the actual subscription of money, there were other ways in which the church or chapel members helped.

---

[1] When the Church was built in 1843 half the cost was met by the L.N.W. Railway and the Radcliffe Trustees.

One of the most outstanding of these is perhaps the efforts that were made in 1907 when the Wolverton Wesleyans re-equipped their school-room. The whole of the building was re-decorated, re-lighted and re-seated, and the various members supplied no less than threequarters of the work involved. It is estimated that 6,674 hours of voluntary work had been put in by seventy-one keen church members.

LOCAL CLERGY

Among the Church of England clergymen in the area at this time were still a few who managed to combine their religious duties with a love of the hunt. From the days when the Rev. Lorraine Smith had been Rector of Passenham, and indeed probably long before, the " Sporting Parson " was quite an institution in the locality. Probably the doyen of them all was the Rev. Kitelee Chandos-Baily, of Old Bradwell, a remarkably handsome man, who had held the living since 1869, and continued to hold it until his death in 1921, thus creating a record of 52 years in the same Vicariate.

Over the border, in Northamptonshire, the tiny parish of Furtho, with its 15 inhabitants, had had as its Rector since 1890 the Rev. J. Payne, who from 1889 to 1893 was also Warden of St. Paul's School, at Stony Stratford. The collapse of the School under his headship, which was said to be due in some measure to the floggings inflicted on the students, by no means deterred him from taking a further part in public activities, for he became the first Parish Chairman of Furtho, and appears to have enjoyed the responsibilities of that office. He died in August 1906, and was succeeded by the Rev. R. S. Mylne, who made the little church very popular. Later on the living was amalgamated with that of Potterspury, and the tiny church of Furtho became less and less used. During the second World War it was used as a repository for precious manuscripts.

At Wicken there was the interesting figure of the Rev. Nelson-Ward, a grandson of Nelson's daughter Horatia. In the Rectory at Wicken were to be seen the most fascinating collection of Nelson and Lady Hamilton relics, which were later on presented to the Royal Maritime Museum at Greenwich.

At Loughton there was the energetic Rev. J. T. Athawes, who had been there since 1883 and was now also Chairman of the Newport Pagnell Rural District Council and Board of Guardians. It was with his help and support that Loughton built four cottages as a memorial to commemorate the Diamond Jubilee of Queen Victoria in 1897, which were let at a rent of 6d. a week.

At Shenley, where the pretty little church had been restored in 1888-90, the Rector for many years was the Rev. Joseph Vincent, whose tendency towards " High Church " practices was remarkable at the time.

Newport Pagnell at the time showed the opposite tendency, for its incumbent from 1904 to 1921 was the Rev. Frederick Gunnery, who was the choice of the Bishop of Oxford, who, as we shall see later, was no lover of " high " church practices.

At Stony Stratford there were now two active churches again : St. Giles, the ancient Chapel of Ease to Calverton, and the newly built Wolverton St. Mary. At St. Giles, the Rev. J. H. Light had recently left for Great Marlow, and was replaced in 1902 by the Rev. Henry Last, who for a quarter of a century enjoyed the respect of the entire locality. He had one pleasant peculiarity ; he would never ride a bicycle, because, as he said, if he cycled his parishioners would never stop and talk to him.

WOLVERTON ST. MARY

It was the newer church of Wolverton St. Mary which was to produce great trouble. It had been built in 1863, and the new parish had been carved out of the older parishes of Wolverton and Calverton. It owed its origin to the Rev. W. P. Trevelyan, Vicar of Old Wolverton from 1856 to 1871 and Rector of Calverton from 1859 to 1881. For many years the new parish was regarded as part of Wolverton. In 1873 St. Mary's Schools were built (now the Plough Inn), and the Parish Room was erected later. It was to this parish that there first came the Rev. D. McKenzie, later Bishop of Zululand, next the Rev. A. W. Mountain, a keen local historian, and in 1885 the founder's son, the Rev. G. P. Trevelyan became the incumbent and ministered to the growing parish until his resignation in 1897. There was now appointed to the " Perpetual Curacy " the Rev. Oliver Partridge Henly, a former pupil of St. Paul's College, Stony Stratford, and an extremely ' high churchman '.

Let us here consider for a moment the Oxford Movement, which was launched in the 1840's by an influential group of young Oxford clergy and students, who startled the calm comfort of the Church of England, with the thesis that she was not

Protestant at all, but Catholic ; and in a series of disturbing and elaborate Tracts, advocated a return to pre-Reformation beliefs, practices, and ceremonial.

In spite of the hubbub they created and the counter-charges of stout Evangelicals who sniffed Popery in every move, these ideas spread. The tide of the Movement had lapped only very gently against the walls of our own local churches until the 1900's, if we except the minor shocks given by the Rev. Corker at St. Giles in the 1870's. Our choirs were nicely surpliced, communion tables were now altars, gleaming with polished brass ; and processions with cross and banners were rather enjoyed—all unthinkable before 1840. But none of these innovations brought much doctrinal change.

Around 1900 an extreme Anglo-Catholic party led by Lord Halifax, pushed ahead from the main stream of the Movement, causing no little stir. It was represented locally by Rev. Joseph Vincent at Shenley, who at great expense, had adorned his church in such magnificence that it became a local wonder. His services were ornate in the extreme, but there was little or no opposition. Perhaps Shenley people rather enjoyed the colour and ceremony, but the people of Stony Stratford were not quite prepared for the same ecclesiastical advances. Within a few years Rev. O. P. Henly of Wolverton St. Mary's had surpassed Shenley in daring, and attracted to his pulpit most of the clerical ' *enfants terrible* ' from every Diocese. For himself, he was a man of singular charm ; a great lover of sport, and in approach frank and direct ; he had little idea of either dissimulation or compromise, and no patience at all with opposition. With these attributes the inevitable happened. He built up a considerable and loyal extreme Anglo-Catholic congregation who adored him, and a hornet's-nest of an opposition who fought incessantly for his removal.

At the passing of the Education Act of 1902, renewed appointments of Foundation Manager and Trustees for St. Mary's Schools became necessary. The Rev. A. G. St. John Mildmay, the new Vicar of Holy Trinity, Old Wolverton, one of the most genial and accommodating of men, was believed to be Manager by Deed of Trust, and since this was contested by the Rev. Henly, the Rev. Mildmay found himself unwittingly leading the first parochial fight. The Rev. Henly's move was brusque and characteristic. On September 24th he closed the schools, announced a holiday for the delighted scholars, and appealed to Aylesbury for confirmation. Promptly came the counter-stroke—the town crier calling around the town that the school would re-open in the morning, and opened it was—after the scaling of gates and the forcing of windows and doors ; but of no avail, as Rev. Henly's claim for control was confirmed by County Authorities ; which opened acrimonious exchanges in the *Wolverton Express*, from which the clergy decently withdrew.

Dr. Paget, then Bishop of Oxford, was caught in the fray two years later, for after reproving the Rev. Henly in 1905 without satisfaction, he brought, in 1906, a suit in the Court of Arches against him for the reservation of the Sacrament, contrary to the Book of Common Prayer, and the Articles of Religion. The Bishop's position was not a happy one ; his own Cathedral City was the very citadel of those practices which the recent Commission on Church discipline had condemned. Oxford was full of clergymen reserving Sacraments, but certain influences which seemed to safeguard them were not in operation at Wolverton St. Mary's. Both the Bishop of Oxford and the Bishop of Reading were called as witnesses, and on December 14th 1906, the Rev. Henly was formally admonished by the Court. For two years there was no further action on the part of the Bishop, but as the local press noted, the Rev. Henly made no change in his ceremonies. In 1909 the suppressed fires burst into new flame, for the Bishop renewed his charges in the Court of Arches against the Rev. Henly, of (i) Reservation of the Sacrament, (ii) Use of certain unauthorized rites and ceremonies, (iii) Disobedience of the monitions of the Court. The Rev. Henly did not appear, neither was he defended by counsel. For the Bishop of Oxford, it was explained that he had written repeatedly to the Vicar of St. Mary's without receiving replies ; that he had seen the Vicar who would say nothing, and that he had asked his resignation without receiving an answer.

In the evidence it appeared that in January 1909 the Archdeacon of Buckingham and the Bishop's Chaplain attended Evensong at St. Mary's. They found a tabernacle with a light burning before it, and after Evensong an Exposition of the consecrated bread taken from the Tabernacle, during which a Litany to the Blessed Virgin was sung, followed by a translation of the Roman Rite of Benediction.

The Dean of Arches then postponed the hearing for fourteen days, in order to give the Vicar of St. Mary's a chance to reconsider his position, but if there was no such reconsideration, there was to be sentence of deprivation of the living, and costs. A fortnight later judgment was formally given, and the Rev. O. P. Henly was deprived " of all his ecclesiastical promotions, and especially of the perpetual curacy or vicarage he enjoyed ". He was also to pay costs.

Meanwhile, Rev. Henly had written a long letter to *The Times* stating that he refused to recognise the court, and that therefore he would not defend the action. He held that reservation of the Sacrament was not forbidden by the laws of the Church, and added that he did not reply to the Bishop's letters because those replies would be used against him.

On Sunday, August 8th, 1909, the Bishop of Oxford arrived at St. Mary's and took all the services that day. At the first early communion service, thirty communicants, led by the Rev. Henly, walked out of the church and marched down to St. Giles to attend the service there. At Matins there was no choir, and no organist. Mr. O. Tyrell volunteered to play the organ but the keys were missing. The Bishop in his sermon made no allusion to recent events.

Five days later, two curates arrived from Oxford, and a police guard headed by Inspector Anthony, of Newport Pagnell, kept the followers of the former Vicar out of the Church. The old locks were removed and new ones fitted. The Rev. Henly was away that day at Brighton, and the crowds grew when it became generally known that he would be returning on the last tram from Wolverton. When the tram arrived he was escorted by a group of supporters to the Vicarage, and there was not a little hustling and booing. The police, however, got him safely through the crowd into the Vicarage, where he was to spend his last week shut out of his former church. On the 20th August, the Bishop preached again, and on August 26th the Rev. Henly left Stony Stratford for ever.

In the January of 1910, the Rev. A. J. Moxon became Vicar of Wolverton St. Mary. He was a young man, full of vigour, with a clean-cut classic face, and soon became well-liked. But his induction produced at least one protest, for Mr. Henly wrote protesting that he was still Vicar. Meanwhile, a cauldron of discontent simmered in the old town. No less than 160 parishioners signed a protest, published in the *Wolverton Express*, alleging that the Bishop had attacked the Holy Sacrament, and had changed the main Sunday service from Mass to morning prayer. The uproar had spread to national Church newspapers, and Wolverton St. Mary, hitherto an obscure little church, was now floodlit in a blaze of contentious publicity.

There was one more unfortunate sequel. The aged verger of St. Mary's, Mr. Edwin Haynes, could not bring himself to go to the church after the Rev. Henly's inhibition, and a few weeks later he was found drowned head first in his own water-butt only a few yards from the Church.

It is all a pitiful story, and what became of it ? The dispersed congregation broke into fragments ; some joined the Roman Catholic Church ; others attached themselves to the more cautious ' high ' church of St. Giles. Father Henly himself retired to Brighton, and was one of the six Brighton Clergy, who with much publicity, ' went over ' to Rome in 1913, followed only shortly afterwards by the curate of St. Giles, the Rev. C. H. Stenson, who joined the Benedictines at Caldy.

After a short Evangelical interlude, St. Mary's returned again to ' high ' church, and today reservation of the Sacrament is the rule rather than the exception in our local churches, which implies that in spite of his condemnation, Father Henly was only a generation ahead of his time.

Neither the strictures of the Bishops, nor the wishes of part of the congregations could prevent the Anglo-Catholic movement within the Church of England from advancing, and within a few years several local churches saw the substitution of the service of the Eucharist for the former Matins, and the gradual re-introduction of elaborate vestments into these services.

This trend was hotly contested by the Kensit preachers, who now began to hold yearly campaigns against the new " ritualism " in the Church of England, and certainly their meetings on the Market Square at Stony Stratford, or near the drinking trough by the "Foresters Arms," were not marked by any lack of heckling or even boisterous pushing on the part of some of the audience.

There were, however, certain churches and Patrons who set themselves stoutly against these " Romish innovations," and principal of them all was the old Duke of Grafton, Lay Rector, and subsequently Patron, of the living of Potterspury, who roundly declared that he was all against " circus antics " in church. When, in 1897, the living of Potterspury fell vacant, he took the very greatest pains to see that the new Vicar was free from suspicion. Whatever the foundations of his choice the new Vicar, the Rev. Walter Plant soon became universally popular.

STANTONBURY ST. JAMES

Yet another church provided problems for Bishops and Parliament alike. In the March of 1909 the newly appointed Vicar of Stantonbury, the Rev. Newman Guest, a typical Irishman, discovered that the Church of St. James' Stantonbury had never been licensed for the solemnisation of marriages. When the church was built in 1850, it was assumed that it took over all the parish responsibilities of the Norman church of St. Peter, which in the olden days had been the centre of the village, then clustered near the Manor House and Mill on the Ouse banks, but New Bradwell had developed a mile or more away, and St. Peter's was left picturesquely alone by the ruins of the Manor House and Mill. In the meantime 434 marriages had taken place at the new church of St. James.

The Rev. Newman Guest had a sense of drama ; for he chose to make the first announcement of the fact that 434 local families were " living in sin " at the end of the evening service one Sunday. The local consternation can be imagined, for there was scarcely a legitimate child in all New Bradwell if the Vicar was right. But right he was ! For weeks there was a touchy atmosphere particularly amongst many who for years had regarded themselves as " respectably married." Naturally immediate steps were taken to improve the situation, and in July the Home Secretary made a provisional order deeming all marriages that had taken place in the church to be valid, and freeing ministers, churchwardens, etc., from any penalty, and later a special Act of Parliament was passed. Great was the relief, but young couples would take no risk, and in the meantime marriages took place at the little Church of St. Peter instead of the suspect St. James.[1]

The Easter Saturday of that year was marked by two weddings, and as can be imagined the unique and romantic character of the proceedings attracted a great deal of interest. The following account of the proceedings is based upon the issue of the

[1] The episode gave rise to a farce which ran for some months at the Criterion Theatre in London, but in the farce the Act of Parliament gave the option to couples married at the unlicensed church to decide whether they should go on being married or not. The actual Act of Parliament for St. James' Church gave no such option.

From a photograph by Mr. J. W. Smith

OLD WOLVERTON CHURCH

And the ancient row of cottages near it in 1902. The cottages were demolished in the 1930's.

Photograph lent by Miss Maguire

WOLVERTON ST. MARY'S CHURCH, STONY STRATFORD, ABOUT 1890

This attractive little church and the adjoining Vicarage was the scene of remarkable incidents in the 1900's which led to the inhibition of the Rev. O. P. Henly. The row of cottages were pulled down about 1895. For the story of the Rev. Henly, see p. 59.

Photograph lent by Mrs. Staley

A PRETTY WEDDING OF 1906

On August 6th 1906 Mr. J. S. S. Staley and Miss Tucker were married at the Orphanage, Stony Stratford, the first wedding which took place in that institution. See p. 68.

Photograph lent by Mrs. Pedder

THE LAST WEDDING AT ST. PETER'S, STANTON LOW

When in 1909 it was suddenly discovered that the Church of St. James at Stantonbury was *not* licensed for marriages (in spite of the fact that hundreds of people had been married there) brides and grooms resorted to the ancient Norman Church at Stanton Low. Our photograph shows Mr. and Mrs. Pedder coming out of the Church. See p. 65.

Northampton Daily Chronicle for that day, and on the memories of Mrs. Pedder who was one of the leading participants in the event.

The day being Easter Saturday, with Wolverton Works closed, many elected to wend their way that morning by way of the towing path, over the fence and across the fields, to the isolated little church. The bridal parties were driven in carriages across the undulating meadows, which were crossed by only the roughest of paths. Everyone was in a boisterous holiday mood, except the principal parties, and one of the flustered brides felt more like crying at the unexpected publicity given to what was meant to be a quiet wedding. The Vicar, the Rev. Newman Guest, was serious too. Half an hour before the first wedding was due he had ordered the burning of incense inside the church " to purify the atmosphere," and by the time the first bridal party arrived he was ready at the head of surpliced choir to lead the procession around the Churchyard whilst they sang " The King of Love my Shepherd is." As they passed through the ancient Norman doorway into the Church " Fight the Good Fight " was sung. There seemed to be a little too much of the holiday spirit about at this moment, for the Vicar turned round and said to the throng : " This is not a beanfeast, but a very solemn occasion."

The first wedding, at 11.30 a.m. was that of Walter Bull, " an intelligent looking young fellow, a native of Stantonbury " and Clara Hawkins, " a fresh looking country girl," and the second that of George Pedder " a skilful young mechanic at Wolverton Works " and Edith Townsend " an attractive young lady residing at Stantonbury." One of our illustrations shows Mr. and Mrs. Pedder coming out of Church after the ceremony. I think this period marks the last beautiful period in the 800 years history of St. Peter's, when these pretty weddings took place in the lovely little church across the fields. After the first World War the little church began to be neglected, and as the years went by its beautiful Jacobean pulpit was kicked in, other woodwork damaged, and even the mediaeval communion table only just rescued in time from complete destruction.

It only remains to add that " Father " Guest soon came to loggerheads with several of the parishioners ; he was an odd type, and there were few in Stantonbury who sympathised with his avowed object of increasing the authority of the priest within the Anglican Church.

On the non-conformist side there were many energetic and lovable men. At Stony Stratford the Rev. Stephen Cheshire was the Pastor of the Baptist flock for 32 years (1893-1925) and a remarkably hard worker in all social causes.

At Wolverton the non-conformists had gone from strength to strength during the past half century. The first Congregational Sunday School, in 1866, was held in a back-room of the North Western Hotel, and as can be imagined, the fifty adult members of the church were anxious to secure other quarters. The Sunday services were held in the old Dining Hall in Stratford Road, by the Rev. T. Coop. In 1874 a site for the chapel was secured at the corner of Radcliffe Street and the Market Square and in 1878 the foundation stone of the chapel was laid. The entire building cost only £830, the builder, Mr. C. Aveline, charging only labour and materials and the members supplying much of the skilled workmanship. In 1889 the present church was begun, and finished a year later at the cost of £1,800, the old chapel becoming the schoolroom. In 1901 there was enlargement, and in the following year the Rev. Henry Welch became the Pastor. He was a most active man, a keen Radical, and extremely interested in all local educational questions. In the same year the Rev. C. Adie Pollard became Pastor of the Wolverton Wesleyan Methodist Church, and, like his Congregational colleague, his activities were many indeed. A Primitive Methodist Church was built at the other end of Church Street in 1907.

THE ORPHANAGE CHAPEL

Side by side with these established churches and chapels, there now came into existence a new one, the extremely Evangelical Chapel connected with Mr. Fegan's Orphanage at Stony Stratford. Half a century earlier, in 1863, the Rev. G. Sankey had built at Stony Stratford a fine public school known as St. Paul's School, but after the death of the founder things never seemed to go right, and in 1896 it was closed. For a short time the buildings became a cigar factory and then for several years remained empty. No one wanted the property. Then, in 1900, it came to the attention of that " Knight Errant of the Gospel," Mr. J. W. C. Fegan, a shrewd business man who had spent his life in helping the homeless boys of London. Fegan was looking for a country home for his " bold and pert and dirty London sparrows ", and his biographer, Dr. W. Y. Fullerton,

Photograph by J. W. Smith

BATH NIGHT AT THE ORPHANAGE BEFORE 1906

In the early days of the Orphanage (Mr. Fegan's Homes) at Stony Stratford the problems of bathing innumerable small boys was partly solved by bathing them in groups of 25 at a time. In 1906 separate baths were introduced. The wooden tub in front was a common object to be found in most homes about this period, and was only replaced in the 1900's by the lighter galvanised iron bath.

Photograph lent by Mr. F. J. Sykes

THE ORPHANAGE BOYS BRIGADE ABOUT 1906

The manifold activities of the Orphanage (Mr. Fegan's Homes) in the 1900's are recounted on p. 66. Among them were the Boys' Brigade and its junior contingent known as "Sykes' Irregulars." Captain F. J. Sykes may be seen seated in the middle.

A TYPICAL INFANTS CLASS OF 1902

The little girls pinafores and the boys' frilly collars add a charming note to this class of 3 to 5 year-olds. Pupil teachers then commenced teaching at 14.

EMPIRE DAY AT WOLVERTON 1909

Empire Day (May 24th) was celebrated throughout the country in the 1900's by parades of school children, patriotic addresses, and fine singing. Our photograph depicts Mr. H. J. Hippsley conducting the singing of the National Anthem.

tells us what happened when Mr. Fegan saw the college :—

> Designed as a school for the sons of gentlemen, the buildings were almost luxurious, everything was of the highest quality, and the whole had cost £40,000. But the school was a failure, the insurance company to whom the property was mortgaged had foreclosed on the estate, and it was difficult to see what could be made of such a property in such a neighbourhood.
>
> "Why not offer a tenth of the cost?" In a spirit of what in the event proved to be divine recklessness, an offer of £4,500 was made, although there seemed scant hope of its acceptance. It was accepted immediately, for it was the only offer made, and a date was set for the completion of the purchase—June 25th, 1900 . . . It seemed impossible to get such a large sum in so short a time . . . but by prayer and picturesque personal letters Mr. Fegan obtained all but £9 by the set day. That night, at a Praise Meeting, an old Christian man living in an almshouse near us made up the amount from his life's savings.

Within a short time 150 bright little fellows from 8 to 11 years of age were brought to "Fegan's Homes", and from that day to this something like 4,000 needy boys have found a home in the buildings that had been intended for boys of quite other fortunes.

The principal for some years was Mr. W. H. Higgins, who retired in 1906, and was succeeded by Mr. W. H. Slade.

In addition to the Home, there was the Chapel, and here Mr. Fegan's evangelical bent had full scope. Services of real heartiness were arranged, and with the help of the Salvation Army the congregation grew so rapidly that the Chapel became too small for the purpose, and great marquees were erected behind the College for the summer revivalist meetings. Mr. Fegan would invite all and sundry to these services. Great speakers and soloists of renown were brought regardless of expense : local non-conformist ministers had the opportunity of addressing greater congregations than ever before. Many converts were made including one Mr. Fegan described as " the worst man in Stratford ". It was hoped that converts might be induced to join the churches in the district, but as the biographer of Mr. Fegan says : "it was inevitable that they should cling to the place where they had received blessing ". Not unnaturally some of the methods used raised the eyebrows of the more formal religious sects and other local congregations suffered great losses in numbers, but Mr. Fegan claimed that he was " bringing souls to Jesus " in no small numbers, and if other congregations were diminishing at any rate their members were to be found at the Orphanage and not at public houses.

All this was helped by Fegan's Boys' Brigade, "under the command of Captain F. C. Sykes," who, by virtue of their smart uniforms and bugling all over the place came to be very well known. The junior group of boys from 6 to 12, very soon acquired the name of " Sykes Irregulars ".

There inevitably came the time when enthusiastic members of the congregation wished to be married in the Orphanage Chapel, and fortunately we have the full details and even charming photographs of the first event of this kind. In order for Miss Millicent May Tucker and Mr. J. S. S. Staley to be married in the Chapel Mr. Fegan had the Chapel licensed, and on August 6th, 1906, the ceremony took place. The local press described it in these words :—

> " At the appointed time the bride and bridegroom, with bridesmaids and friends, entered the Chapel. After the singing of the hymn ' Ten thousand thanks to Jesus ' prayer was offered by Mr. J. Wharton, and then Mr. Fegan read portions of the Scripture relating to marriage. The marriage form was then gone through, and a few words of counsel and advice given by Mr. Fegan, and the company repaired to the dining hall to partake the refreshments so generously provided for them. The bride wore a handsome dress of cream voile, trimmed with lace, a veil with wreath of orange blossom, and carried a shower bouquet of flowers in her hand. In the afternoon the happy group were photographed in the school-yard ".

Among the presents was a heavy black clock from Mr. Fegan, of which there were only five like it in the whole country.

One of the photographs which we are fortunate in being able to reproduce shows the truly charming bride, with a 20-inch waist, leg of mutton sleeves, up-swept hair and an extremely pleasant look.

THE ROMAN CATHOLICS

Of the Catholics there is little to say. They were not indigenous to our countryside excepting at Weston Underwood, where, under the protection of the Throckmortons they had been privileged to form an enclave since Elizabethan days, thus escaping the rigorous penal laws operating elsewhere. Most local County families and College Corporations had been created or enriched by the Reformation, so Roman Catholics on their estates were not only unwelcome ; they just ceased to exist.

The little congregation at Wolverton came, in the main, with the railway influx in the 1840's. Weston Underwood being inaccessible, Mass was said for them at the Radcliffe Arms which stood near the old Market Hall. A church—" St. Francis of Sales " was built by a private donor in 1867. It is a plain but substantial building, accommodating easily the congregation of 100 at the beginning of the century. In 1902, the energetic Father Garnett, as Priest in Charge, became a popular town personality, succeeded in 1905 by Father O'Sullivan, and later by Father Walker.

The Catholic community are a paradox. Whilst all denominations were expanding and enlarging their churches and halls, they remained static, but when church-going slumped elsewhere, they began to gain ground. At the end of the decade a community of teaching nuns purchased Thornton Hall for a Girls' College. They not only preserved this historic house from an unknown fate, but have achieved considerable success in their venture. Later, Mr. and Mrs. G. Beale, of Potterspury Lodge, built an Oratory dedicated to the Sacred Heart, to serve their estate and the scattered Catholics of those parts. With the shifting of population, and many individual conversions, the local Catholics very soon doubled and even trebled their numbers.

The Roman Catholic Church was probably the only one which during the next generation made actual gains in its congregation. For the rest, the growing secularisation of Sunday, the wireless, and Sunday games, did much to destroy the Victorian Sunday of our forefathers, but at the time of which we are writing the Victorian Sunday was a very real event. In those days scarcely a vehicle passed down the length of the Stony Stratford High Street on the Sabbath. Only five trains stopped at Wolverton on that day. Cynics have said that people went to Church then because there was nothing else to do—or simply to see the new hats at Eastertime—but this is very far from the truth. Most people went to church because they liked it, and because they found a great spiritual satisfaction in what they regarded as the proper use of the Lord's Day.

CHURCH PARADES

Occasionally there were special occasions when, large as the churches were, they could not contain all those who wished to come to the service. Both at Wolverton and at Stony Stratford there were the annual Church Parades of the local volunteers, when every seat was taken, and latecomers had to be content with either standing crowded together at the west end or to listen to the service from outside. These parades made a brave show. In those days khaki was only used in the field, and for Church parades the volunteers appeared in all the glory of rifle grey piped with scarlet or blue piped with scarlet, surmounted by the spiked metal tipped helmet or busby and plume that made every man look a foot taller. At Stony Stratford the R.A.M.C. parade was under the command of Colonel W. H. Bull, who, in his cocked hat (actually surmounted by green, black and gold cock's feathers) brilliant uniform, medals, and the glittering sword, was all that any small boy could ever expect any General to look like.

At these church parades the usual combination of organ and choir was replaced by the local military or town band, since local organs and bands were never attuned to the same pitch. Churches were really made for such music, and to hear "*The Old Hundredth*" or "*Onward Christian Soldiers*" sung by several hundred men's voices led by a superb choir and a good silver band, was something never to be forgotten.

Other occasions when the churches were crowded were of course on the occasions when the Bishop of Oxford came for the confirmation service, and at Eastertime and Christmas, but at these services the stridency of brass was replaced by the softer tones of the organ, and the trebles could be heard to much greater advantage.

One of the traits of this period, which had now unfortunately almost disappeared, was the ability of most people to sing entire hymns through without looking at the book, and to quote correctly many passages from the Bible or Shakespeare. The catechism was of course learned by heart at all Church of England schools, but this was only one example of "learning by rote", for in the 1900's many elementary schoolchildren learned long passages from "*The Merchant of Venice*" and other Shakespearean plays.

This practice unquestionably helped to train the memory, but it also had another curious effect, for on the great occasions when a Church was full to the overflowing, and there were not enough hymn-books to go round for those who had not brought them, it was no uncommon sight to see and hear hundreds of Volunteers all singing "*Onward Christian Soldiers*" from memory with a unanimous vigour.

It was the same at the Orphanage, where at this time great meetings were held in huge marquees erected behind the old school. The great revivalist hymns were all known by heart, and the favourites like *"Oh, that will be glory for me"* or *"Abide with Me"* were sung with uplifted eyes and a fervour that came from the heart.

In many ways this memorisation may have been a relic from the times when few could read, and in order to be able to take part in a church service knowledge of the prayer or hymn-book through memory was essential, but it came out in so many other ways. Some of our local carriers and even town criers were illiterate, but given the message no matter what the interval of time before its delivery, they would repeat it exactly. Messages cost a penny to deliver, but long ones were tuppence.

Town criers were of course as important as the radio is to-day. Mostly their pronouncements were of the " Lost, Stolen or Strayed " order, or notifications about the gas or water supply, but occcasionally they would be used to advertise meet-ings, or an enterprising tradesman would thus indicate the arrival of some new merchandise, and on one occasion at least as we have seen the Vicar of Old Wolverton used the town crier to cry that the schools would be open after the Vicar of St. Mary's had shut them.

CHAPTER VI

Politics and Education

" That every boy and every gal,
That's born into the world alive,
Is either a little liberal
Or else a little conservative ".

SO SANG PRIVATE WILLIS in Gilbert and Sullivan's opera
" Iolanthe ", and it was certainly true of Wolverton and Stony
Stratford in the 1900's. Politics were in fact as hereditary
as religion, though the previous generation had been shocked
by a great transfer of " Liberal Unionists " to the Conservative
cause in the 1880's.

These hereditary leanings or preferences apparently had no
economic foundation, for entire streets could be found where
red alternated with blue ; but it did apparently have some
connection with religious beliefs, though here again there
seemed to be very little difference economically or socially
between those who were non-conformists or those who were
Church of England.

Whichever party one supported, enthusiasm was probably
much greater than is observable to-day. Obviously in the
1900's no-one could sit quietly at home listening, over the
radio, to the voice of the Prime Minister, or the Leader of the
Opposition, or other important statesman. To attend meetings
was the only way to listen in, and meetings were attended to a
degree which is seldom realised to-day. But meetings were infrequent, since the only method of transport sure and safe was
still the horse and trap, and it would take a couple of hours to
get from Buckingham to Newport, or from Olney to Linslade,
which then, as now, were in the Buckingham Division. It
was not only at meetings that enthusiasm or dislike was demon-
strated, for political keenness then showed itself in many curious
forms. In the 1900 election, for example, at Stony Stratford
two outstanding protagonists, the one a Conservative and the
other a Liberal, both found that strange things had been done
to their houses. Mr. Keveren, who lived at 15 London Road,

woke up one morning to find his house plastered with Liberal bills and slogans, while Mr. Swinfen Harris, who lived at 107, High Street, found that his house had been sprayed or spattered with tar. The marks show to-day. Window breaking and damaging gardens too was not an infrequent occurrence. Indeed it was not until after the first world war that there began to appear the rudiments of tolerance in politics.

As for airing one's opinion, in the 1900's it was done with much greater gusto than to-day, and not infrequently Saturday night political discussions at the local ended up with fisticuffs. Drunken enthusiasts sought to settle the fates of empires by giving each other a bloody nose.

PARLIAMENTARY ELECTIONS

The Buckingham division at the period was represented in Parliament by the popular figure of Mr. Walter Carlile, of Gayhurst, who had first been returned for the division in 1895 with a majority of 436 over Sir Herbert Leon, which in those days was considered not at all bad since only male freeholders, or those with lodging qualifications, were allowed to vote, and every year there were the most minute enquiries into the admissibility of anyone on to the electoral list, consequently there were only 11,000 electors in the whole constituency. In 1900, Mr. Carlile stood again, and had the satisfaction of maintaining his majority against the Hon. Hubert Beaumont with the loss of only a score of votes.

By 1903 the Liberals had regained much of their lost confidence, and were determined with their new candidate, Mr. F. W. Verney, to upset the Tories. As for the Tories, Mr. Carlile had announced his intention of not standing again, and in his place the Conservatives had chosen the Hon. T. F. Fremantle, whose father, Lord Cottesloe, had been M.P. for Bucks from 1876 to 1885. Mr. Fremantle had been Assistant Secretary to the Secretary of State for War from 1900 to 1903, he was an expert on the rifle, and lived at Swanbourne.[1]

When the election came early in 1906 both parties were more than ready for a very stiff fight.

Many of the meetings of the campaign that followed were broken up or abandoned in scenes of disorder. At Castlethorpe

---

[1] He succeeded his father as third Baron Cottesloe in 1918.

the Conservative Candidate, Mr. Fremantle, was enthusiastically received, but at Hanslope " the answers of the Candidate were " so satisfactory that the Radicals present wished to hear no " more, and amid a scene of disorder the Hon. T. F. Fremantle " departed ".

In those days various constituencies polled on different days, thus the full results of the election were not known until a fortnight after the first returns were to hand. It was therefore extremely probable that the earlier returns greatly influenced the later ones. The Buckingham Division was among the late middle batch, and when on the Monday it became known that the Liberals had captured Northampton, Bedford and Cambridge, and by the Wednesday had captured 67 seats from the Tories, there were increasing hopes that Verney would beat Fremantle, and Liberal predictions of a thousand majority were frequent.

On the Friday, January 19th, 1906, North Bucks polled, and the result was :—

Verney	...	...	...	6,253
Fremantle	...	...	...	4,673
Liberal Majority		...		1,580

Such an enormous majority had never been known in the Buckingham Division before. The Liberals were ecstatically happy ; the Conservative naturally chagrined. At Buckingham, where the poll was declared, Mr. Verney could not be heard, and had to return to his temporary residence at Maids Moreton without being able to offer a single word of congratulations to his supporters. But it was different when he arrived at Wolverton that afternoon, when he addressed a large crowd from the windows of Mr. Davies' house in the Stratford Road. As for Stantonbury, it went wild with joy.

At Stony Stratford the result was received with very mingled feelings. The Cock Hotel was the Conservative headquarters, but so intense was the enthusiasm of some Conservative supporters that houses were literally plastered with bills, placards, and slogans, some of which would now be considered almost libellous. Nos. 26 and 28 High Street for instance (formerly the historic Rose and Crown Inn) had no less than 33 such bills. After the declaration of the poll some of the Liberal residents had their windows broken, while Mr. Coop, a respected tradesman who lived at the White Lodge, Wolverton Road (now the Bus Office), had his gates taken off their hinges, smashed, and thrown into an adjoining field whilst his shrubs and flowers were pulled up. Mr. David Jones, of Old Stratford, one of the finest schoolmasters in the area, and a very left wing Radical, was subjected to similar affront.

Meanwhile the victorious Verney had visited the town, the Town Band was engaged, and to the strains of "*See the Conquering Hero Comes*" he was escorted to Mr. Hall's house near the top of the town. After making a short speech of thanks he was played on his way to thank other supporters in other towns and villages.

One of our local reporters asked the defeated Conservative candidate the tactless question : " Why did you lose ? " the answer came : " Partly Chinese labour and education. Mainly Conservative collapse elsewhere ".

One of the oddest things about these elections was that although both the telegraph and telephone were now installed locally, the first results usually came by cycle up to 1906. The racing cyclists of the local cycling clubs were then faster than any other method then known of spreading the news. But in that year telephones were installed at Wolverton and Stony Stratford, and there were fifteen private lines put in mostly of course to hotels and business premises.

There is one odd note in our researches into the political history of this area. By and large, political discussion was orderly, even if it did become a little heated on Saturday nights in the public houses, especially when elections were in the offing. But there was one public meeting at which there were over a hundred police and stewards determined to keep order —without being able to claim a complete success. The main subjects of political discussion at this time were broadly Free Trade versus Tariff Reform, and the Education Acts, but a group of ladies had introduced a new theme " Votes for Women", and even as early as 1909 they were adopting methods which were certainly original.

When, therefore, the Liberal Prime Minister, Mr. H. H. Asquith, came to Bletchley Park to speak in the August of 1909, tremendous preparations were made to ensure that these " wild women " did not hit him with their umbrellas, or chain themselves to the railings, or even throw themselves under the Prime Minister's carriage. The suffragettes were, however, cleverer than the police, for one at least chained herself to a tree in the Park, while others with speaking trumpets shrilled out : " Votes for Women " even while the Prime Minister was speaking. There was a stiff skirmish, several ladies were locked up for a few hours, and the meeting went on free from further interruption.

In the year 1910 there were two general elections, an event unprecedented in English history, and as can be imagined election fever ran high during the entire year. It may be well to recall that the Liberal Party headed by the Prime Minister, the Rt. Hon. H. H. Asquith, and the dynamic Chancellor of the Exchequer, the Rt. Hon. David Lloyd George, had embarked upon great measures of social reform, some of which met with opposition from the House of Lords, which then had much greater power than to-day. In the January 1910 election the North Bucks result was :—

F. W. Verney	...	...	6,055
T. F. Fremantle	...	...	5,941
Liberal Majority		...	111

It was a close squeak, and the Liberals went back to power with a majority of 1 over the Conservatives, but the 41 Labour and 71 Nationalist members gave them a good working majority. Ten months later Liberal difficulties with the House of Lords led Mr. Asquith to ask the new King, George V, for a dissolution. The result was no change, for both in England generally and in Bucks in particular the various parties achieved about the same results. But in North Bucks not with the same men, for early in 1910 Mr. F. W. Verney, whose health was now failing decided to contest the more compact borough of Bournemouth, and his nephew Sir Harry Verney, fourth Baronet and a large landowner, was chosen as the Liberal standard bearer in his stead. On the Conservative side, the Hon. T. F. Fremantle gave way to Col. F. T. H. Bernard, of Chearsley Hill, but this made little difference to the result, for Sir Harry Verney was returned with a majority of 327, and was destined to remain the Member for North Bucks until 1918. There were over 100 police at the declaration of the poll at Buckingham, but even this force could not prevent some ugly rushes and some egg throwing.

Behaviour throughout the elections was little better than in 1900 or 1906 elections, and there was " too much hooliganism at Wolverton " when Mr. Fremantle held a meeting there. It was, in fact a scene of continuous rowdyism, even the doors were broken, and Lord Desborough with his loud booming voice was the only speaker who could be heard at all. It was estimated that both the Conservative and Liberal candidates in North Bucks had spent nearly £2,000 each fighting the two elections in 1910—nearly twelve times as much in money values as is allowed to be spent now-a-days.

Sir Harry Verney's maiden speech in the House of Commons was one of the most curious ever made. By some incredible error he had been returned as " Sir Harry Calvert Williams ", the returning clerk having forgotten to add his surname, and it was no little shock to Sir Harry to find on taking the oath that he was so described. That day he caught the Speaker's eye, and to an astonished and amused house explained that " Verney's the name, not Williams ".

Another interesting circumstance of the time was the dubiety with which this locality received the first exponents of socialism. Possibly the first socialist in the area was Mr. David Jones, the energetic schoolmaster of the British School at Stony Stratford, who as early as 1906 was lecturing on topics such as " Can a Socialist be Virtuous ? " In July 1907 the *Wolverton Express* in a leading article refers non-committally to the growth of the Labour Party in England, and in the August there was the first Labour meeting in the open air at the Tram Terminus—or what is now the bus stop—at Stony Stratford.

The first public mention of the nationalisation of the railways in the area was in a speech delivered by the Liberal M.P. Sir Leo Chiozza Money, at the Science and Art Institute at Wolverton in that year.

In Wolverton and in New Bradwell there were a few who openly sympathised with the new Labour movement, but in the main held that it was part and parcel of liberalism. The Amalgamated Society of Railway Servants (later to be merged into the National Union of Railwaymen) included several of these, but there seems to have been a determination not to get too deeply into politics. It was rather a friendly society with an industrial bias, and one of its best known activities was the Annual Parade, with the banners of the Wolverton and Bletchley branches, and the Newport Prize and Bradwell United bands, through the towns of the area, collecting for the Railway Orphanage.

THE EDUCATION ACT OF 1902

Of all the political questions of the day, none perhaps caused more discussion and heartburning than the Education Act of 1902. Broadly speaking, it laid the foundation of popular education as we know it to-day. It gave local authorities power to provide assistance to voluntary schools, and also facilities for secondary and technical schools, and was a long step in the direction of creating a literary nation, but it was bitterly opposed by the non-conformists, who objected to paying the newly-imposed education rate, since they were already paying for the British schools to which most non-conformist children went. In July 1903 a Passive Resistance Society was formed the aim of which was to refuse to pay any such rates, and indeed to prefer prison to payment.

In Stony Stratford two dozen passive resisters refused a l attempts to get them to pay. Finally, in January 1904, there was held the first of many sales of the personal goods of these resisters, after distress warrants had been issued by the Police. The actual rate was a relatively small sum, rarely amounting to more than a few shillings, but for the next ten years, and even longer in some cases, our leading Free Churchmen underwent this continued process of distress warrant, and sale, in order to protest against what they regarded as a sectarian measure. The names of the resisters include many who have since done yeoman service to the locality, several subsequently serving on the local councils and helping their fellow citizens in a hundred and one ways. Heading the list were Mr. F. W. Woollard, C.C., and Mr. Ulph Woollard, then came Mr. T H. Calladine, Mr. H. S. Perrin, Mr. J. W. Smith, the Rev. Stephen Cheshire, Mr. Arthur Barley, Mr. B. Bridgeman, Mr. A. Hall, and Mr. G. Benson, all of Stony Stratford ; then came Mr. C. Ball, Mr. J. Barnes, Mr. W. H. Coleman, Mr. W. H. Hopkins, Mr. Pelham Howell, Mr. W. H. Hunt, Mr. W. G. S. Hutchinson, Mr. A. B. Johnson, Mr. Thomas Keene, Mr. Edward Kitchener, the Rev. H. Welch, and the Rev. C. H. Spivey, of Wolverton, and finally Mr. W. Foddy, of Wolverton St. Mary's. Three more came from Fenny Stratford. The sale attracted one of the largest crowds ever seen in the Market Square. A farm wagon formed the auctioneer's rostrum, and the gavel was wielded by one who was himself a passive resister—Mr. Thomas Osborne from Buckingham. The proceedings, which were good-humoured

Photograph by Thorneycroft

WOLVERTON WORKS FIRE BRIGADE IN THE 1900's
A delightful action photograph taken during a practice run. See p. 95.

Photograph lent by Mr. Compton

THE RESULT OF THE FIRE AT CASTLETHORPE 1905
A spark from a train set a stable and thirteen houses on fire. See p. 95.

Photograph lent by Mr. F. S. Woollard

STONY STRATFORD'S FOOTBALL TEAM 1907-8

One of the finest teams Stratford ever turned out, and which won both the Buckingham and Ascott League Championships in that year. See p. 101.

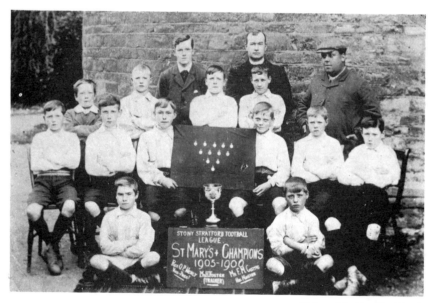

Photograph lent by Miss Maguire

WOLVERTON ST. MARY'S SCHOOL FOOTBALL TEAM 1905-6

The Champion school team of that year, whose story is told on p. 103. Standing at the back can be seen the figure of the Rev. O. P. Henly, whose story is told on p 59 seq.

and indeed humorous in parts, were opened by a speech from Mr. Osborne, who surveying the mingled watches, tea pots, cruets, toast racks, etc., which had been distrained by the Police, remarked that his sympathies were all with those whose goods he was selling : " We are determined to suffer, and to suffer quietly, but still to make our protest . . . All the great reforms from Magna Charta onwards had been made by those who were willing to suffer. Sooner or later the obnoxious Act would be altered or amended, or destroyed altogether ". He then announced that the total amount required was £9 8s. 2d. so that he would put all the goods up together in one lot, and " would be pleased if someone would bid for them ". After a moment's silence, Mr. J. S. Tibbetts, grocer, congregationalist and councillor, who sat on the wagon, made the desired bid. No one else spoke. Mr. Osborne raised his gavel—" Going— going—gone ! "

Everybody was surprised, for the non-conformists had arranged amongst themselves that Mr. Pelham Howell, of Wolverton, was to bid for the goods, and to re-sell (at rate value) to their original owners ; and Mr. Tibbetts' action upset everybody, but the goods were soon restored to their respective owners.

Short speeches followed, condemning the Education Act, but within a quarter of an hour all was over, and " the crowd dispersed as quietly as a congregation leaving the church ".

Every few months similar sales took place for years afterwards. Not until the first World War was in full spate did the non-conformists relent in their determination to resist the Education Act of 1902 by every lawful means within their power.

The new Education Act however greatly increased literacy throughout the country, but it is rather surprising to consider how many schools there were in this neighbourhood even before the passing of the Act. Stony Stratford's best school, St. Paul's College, had ceased to function in 1896, and nothing had really taken its place, though up the London Road was an excellent school (boarding and day) run by Mrs. Slade and her daughter (York House School), which catered for the smaller boys and young ladies.

LOCAL SCHOOLS

Apart from Slade's, there were no less than three elementary schools, the British School, at the top of the town, built in

1844, which was entirely non-conformist in finance and doctrine, whilst the Church of England could claim both St. Giles' Schools in the High Street, and St. Mary's Schools in the buildings which are now the Plough Inn. The writer can well remember his first days as a three-year-old in the latter school, and being taught to fold a piece of coloured paper in two, and learning to sing " *God Save the Queen* ", though the Queen had been dead for sometime—but that was what the music was entitled and what the children sang. The days always began and ended with prayers, and the scrubbed wooden floors were very hard on the tender bare knees of little children.

The Church schools continued separately until 1908, when St. Giles became the Boys' School and St. Mary's, the Girls'.

Up to about 1905 all schools were for preference built along the main highways, it meant completely clean going for the children ; but after that date it was realised that to have a school along the High Street or Stratford Road was extremely dangerous. Children released from school catapulted out on to the highway, and in spite of frequent safety lectures by the teachers, accidents would happen. In the 1900's all four of Stratford's schools and Wolverton's elementary were on the main highway, to-day not one is so sited.

The teachers were remarkable, and not one who went to school in those days will ever forget the efficiency of kindly school mistresses of the type of the Misses Amos, Hayes, Keveren, Plumb or Underwood. Miss Fryer was headmistress at Stony Stratford Church schools until 1924.

In Wolverton education had been, since about 1839, the peculiar care of the Railway Company. In 1840 the first school was built on the site of the present Market Hall, and was surrounded by a small court and garden. There were about 180 pupils. In 1896 a better designed Boys' School was built in what were then the fields to the west of the town, and a girls' and infants' school followed later. It was of the Boys' School that Mr. B. Franklin was head for 30 years.

Meanwhile the need for secondary education was becoming more and more acute. In 1901 the Rev. Soames, Vicar of Lavendon, was Chairman of the Bucks Education Committee, and supported by Mr. Wylie, Mr. Woollard, and others from Wolverton and district he soon got a scheme approved for what was later to become the Grammar School.

Photograph lent by Mrs. Lawman

THE FLOWER SHOW AT LATHBURY PARK

Flower shows were tremendously popular in the 1900's, and the Lathbury show was one of the most popular, for over 2,000 people attended annually. In the background can be seen the great marquees, Billings Roundabouts, Thurston's Switchbacks and all the fun of the fair. See p. 108.

Photograph lent by Mrs. E. J. Dickson

" DARKTOWN " AT STANTONBURY IN 1900

" The Darktown Charity Organisation " was a remarkable mixture of nigger minstrels, clowns, bands, etc., which raised a great deal of money for charity. See p. 110.

In the January of 1902 the " Wolverton County Day School " held its first classes in the Science and Art Institute. There were two forms only since there were only 32 pupils. Mr. L. H. Leadley, B.A., B.Sc., was the first Head, and the terms were 35s. per term, books and stationery included. The first speech day was held on December 19th, 1902 ; and the list of prizewinners includes the name of " Stanley Woollard, 2nd form, for general proficiency ", and the programme concluded with a violin solo by the same young spark who was subsequently destined to become Chairman of the Wolverton U.D.C.

The School continued at the Science and Art Institute for several years, and it was not until October 1906 that new buildings were ready for a school which had by then increased to over 100 pupils. The new buildings, on one of the healthiest sites in Wolverton, cost £6,000, but within two years they were inadequate to house the ever-growing number of pupils.

At Stantonbury, the Council School, originally a Voluntary School, had been opened in 1863 with 50 scholars. In 1867 Mr. George Howitt became the Headmaster; in all he served for 44½ years in the same school before he retired in 1908, after seeing something like 3,000 boys pass through his hands. It was during his mastership that the school was extended in 1891 and 1906, and when he left the school was one of the largest in Bucks with 900 scholars. It was also for many years the model school for Buckinghamshire.

One of the masters who began his career here, Mr. H. J. Hippsley, was to achieve greater renown as Headmaster in Wolverton, where at the Council School he supervised the training of thousands of boys until his retirement in 1921.

The new Elementary Schools at Wolverton were completed in October 1906, and the old schools became the Market Hall.

Meanwhile the Secondary School had been extended in 1908, and could now boast of 135 scholars. The new " Boss ", the bustling, bristling, industrious and most respected E. J. Boyce, was rapidly raising its standard year by year, and it was soon challenging the very best in the country.

New schools were now being rapidly built. In October 1907 the new Council Schools at Stony Stratford were opened, they had cost £4,300, not a small sum in those days. The old British School closed down for ever.

THE SCIENCE AND ART INSTITUTE

Of all the educational institutions in Wolverton at this period, none evoked greater affection than the Science and Art Institute, where the beloved and efficient Mr. R. King was Secretary for 42 years, from 1871 to 1913. It had its origins perhaps as early as June 1st 1840, when local railwaymen, on their own initiative held a meeting and resolved that a Society be formed to be called " The London and Birmingham Railway Institute for moral and intellectual improvement at the Wolverton Station ". On June 15th the Institute was opened in a single room, and a few months later 100 books were bought. In 1843 the first evening classes and lectures were held. In 1861 the Railway Company gave a site in Church Street for a proper building, and on Whit-Monday 1864 it was opened under the name of the Science and Art Institute. The building included a dozen class-rooms, a library, a lecture room, and a music hall, and a second hall was added in 1891. For many years the Institute was the exciting centre of social and cultural life in Wolverton. Lectures, concerts, balls and parties were innumerable, and the library was well stocked with works of all the best authors. But naturally its main function was the teaching through the evening classes. As a pupil for four years at this excellent night school I remember nostalgically the faint musty odour of the class-rooms ; that aroma of pine wood and chalk which nothing ever seems to eradicate. Most of the pupils were as keen as mustard, and I have to confess with a sort of ashamed grin that I was the only one to be expelled from the school. It was Mr. T. Cadwallader (who succeeded Mr. King), who with gentle gruffness told me to remove myself in 1914. Others, much more serious in their studies, and less inclined to frivolous pranks, went on to fame, and the Honours Board in the Reading Room bears testimony to the many who won scholarships to universities or other distinctions.

In the years before the first World War there were over 500 scholars, most of whom naturally studied subjects connected with the railway, such as engineering in its many forms, but there was also the arts side, where shorthand, bookkeeping and French were taught.

In 1925 a Junior Technical School was opened here, promoted in 1926 to be a Technical College. New laboratories were erected and equipped but even to-day it is still unequal from the point of view of accommodation to meet the demands of the many who still want vocational training.

There is unfortunately no full list of the men and women of this area who have achieved success in serving their fellows, but any such list would include distinguished generals like Sir John Nixon, famous professors like Dr. Ernest Coker, leading comedy actors like George Grossmith, many distinguished engineers, architects and schoolmasters, directors of famous companies, learned historians, Mayors of several important towns, and a Member of Parliament. The quality of the human product of the area during the 1900's was unquestionably high, and for that praise must surely be given to the pastors and masters who moulded the plastic and ebullient youth of the period.

LOCAL GOVERNMENT

Local government in these days was not greatly different in manner from that existing to-day. Wolverton and Stony Stratford were then combined in a Rural District Council, and were the leading authority in the district, for County Councils had then by no means the authority and power they have to-day. For many years Mr. G. M. Fitzsimons was the Chairman. On the County Council, Stony Stratford was represented for years by Mr. F. W. Woollard, who was one of the original members when the County Council was set up in 1891. After his death in 1910 he was followed by Mr. J. S. Tibbetts. At Wolverton, the County Council elections were hotly contested, and perhaps the keenest contest of all came in 1907, when Mr. F. W. Verney, then the Liberal M.P. for North Bucks, and former County Councillor, stood as the Liberal and Radical candidate, and the equally popular Dr. J. Owen Harvey, stood, as the Ratepayers' candidate. It had, as the local press said all the excitement of a general election, and when the result was announced there was general jubilation in the Conservative camp which had supported Dr. Harvey, for he squeezed in by a majority of 124 after a heavy poll. Three years later he defeated Mr. W. Purslow by a majority of 138.

Each parish then had its parish council, and Stony Stratford still had two, for the ancient parishes of Stony Stratford East (St. Mary Magdalene) and West (St. Giles) were still separated by the Watling Street, and somehow nobody was very keen on their uniting.

For many years the Rev. Stephen Cheshire was Chairman of the West side, and on one occasion at least that Council seriously considered what it could do to stop the youths of the town from lounging at the tram corner!

Some of the parish council elections saw no less than a dozen candidates, and sometimes the candidate at the bottom of the poll received less than a dozen votes out of hundreds.

A great part of Stony Stratford, in fact the whole area between Wolverton Road and London Road, was in the parish of Wolverton St. Mary, and included for rates and everything else in Wolverton. Calverton Road, and its offshoots, including Park Road, and the newly built " Augusta " Road, as it was originally called, were known as Calverton End and in Calverton Parish.

There were curious differences in the rates, according to the parish. Wolverton was lowest with 5s. 11d. in the £, whilst the two Stratford parishes were nearly twice as high at 8s. 10d. (East) and 9s. 2d. (West). Calverton was 6s. 5d. in the £.

The Stony Stratford and Wolverton Rural District Council then had a rateable value of £52,000 and an almost minute staff. The Medical Officer of Health for the Stony Stratford and Wolverton Sanitary District was the popular Irish born Dr. T. S. Maguire (more often known as " Paddy " Maguire), and during his tenure of office he had the satisfaction of seeing the infantile mortality rate go down from 120 per 1,000 to under 58. He was one of the keenest advocates of water and sewage schemes and there is no doubt that he had the keen satisfaction of being a social reformer who saw the good results of his efforts in his own lifetime.

It was in 1911 that the first indication came of a desire to change the Rural District into an Urban District. In the February of that year there was a meeting to discuss the possibility of Urban powers for Wolverton and Mr. W. J. C. Ray, a townsman with a great record of service in the volunteers, the territorials and in the law, proposed that there should be an Urban District Council for Stony Stratford and Wolverton. After considerable discussion the motion was lost. But the move was on, and in 1919 Mr. Ray's dream took effect.

THE MARKET SQUARE

There was another subject which occasioned quite a lot of discussion locally in the 19th century, and that was the question as to whom the Market Square belonged? It had been a sort of belief that it belonged to the town, and certainly since time immemorial it had been looked after by the ancient Bridge and Street Charity the origins of which are lost in antiquity. This Charity had an income of £200 a year from bequests of certain worthies by the name of White and Marshe, to which was added a bequest of " 20 nobles yearly to repair the highways for ever " by Sir Simon Bennet in 1632. By an Act of Parliament of 1801 these charities were brought together under the control of the Stony Stratford Street Commissioners. Great was their surprise therefore when in 1860 they learnt that the then Lord of the Manor of Calverton and Stony Stratford West Side (Mr. Selby Lowndes) had sold a part of the Market Square in order that the Police Station might be built upon it. They, as Trustees for the Public, promptly wrote to the Lord of the Manor that "although Mr. Lowndes may have the soil vested in him, and is entitled to take tolls on fair days and abridge the rights of the public, the Market Square ought not to be appropriated and the rights of the public excluded ". The reply from the steward of the manor was to the point : " There can be no doubt that, the Market Square belongs to Mr. Lowndes as lord of the manor and he can do what he pleases with it. He has always paid the land tax and outgoings for it, and there can be no question about it. I never before heard of the title being disputed ".

This, when it became public, was a real shock to the town. There was, of course, no question as to who owned the various houses in or around the Square, and it was thought that the inns owned their respective " yards ", but it had been generally supposed that whilst the lord of the manor had the right to take tolls on market-days, he could not sell the actual land for building purposes. It did not need much imagination to see that the whole square could be sold to a local builder, and that one of our best amenities in the way of an open space could be completely built over. There were many who said that the square belonged to the town, and in any case it was the Street Commissioners who had had to pay for the erection of the railings for the cattle market in 1888 and who paid for surfacing from time to time.

For a generation the question hung fire, and in 1901 it seemed as if the happy solution had been reached when William Selby Lowndes sold to the Stratford Street Commissioners " All and every his manorial rights in or over the said Market Square, the said Street called Silver Street, and the said Horse Fair

Green adjoining ". But twelve years later, when the old Act of 1801 was repealed and the Street Commissioners deputed most of their responsibilities to the Parish Council as Trustees, the question was raised again, and when the Urban District Council took over a few years later it was decided to take legal opinion on the legality of the 1901 deed and subsequent happenings. Fortunately, counsel's opinion justified the deed, and in 1931 the Street Commissioners handed over to the U.D.C. all their rights on the Market Square, excepting only that they retained the right to maintain Wesley's elm-tree, the right to provide for the parking of private cars, to hold a fat stock show, and to carry out repairs to the Market Square. The site of Jeffs cottage (demolished in 1906) which had hitherto belonged to the Commissioners, was also handed over to the U.D.C. And that is the situation at the moment, so far as we know, and it might be said that the last rights of the lord of the manor are held by the democratically elected urban district council. But the Street Commissioners still retain one or two of the privileges first allowed to Hugh de Vere, Earl of Oxford, in 1257 by Henry III.

CHAPTER VII

Health and Sanitation

IN THESE DAYS OF National Health schemes there is a tendency to think that before these schemes came into being very few received adequate medical treatment, but the fact is that there was not very much difference in the actual attention doctors gave to patients then compared with to-day. In every town or large village there were two organisations which looked after the sick and infirm—the Provident Dispensaries and the Friendly Societies. At Wolverton, for example, there was the Wolverton and Stantonbury Dispensary, run by Dr. Charles Miles, which for the sum of 1s. per family per month provided medical attention and medicine without further charge, whilst at Stony Stratford, the Provident Dispensary, established in 1866 along-side the Cottage Hospital on the Green, had a similar system. Nearly every working-class family in the area belonged to the one or the other of these Dispensaries ; but most of the trades-men and well-to-do were the direct private patients of the doctor of their choice.

The Provident Dispensaries, however, did not cover hospital services, and to secure these it was necessary to belong either to a Friendly Society or to a Hospital Association. The Friendly Societies, in addition to this field of endeavour, also provided sick-pay for those of their members who were unable to work through sickness. All this was done with remarkably little fuss or bother, and without anything other than a mildly bene-volent approval from Whitehall. Then, as now, no doctor ever refused to go to a bed of sickness or to an accident because the patient was not duly enrolled with the appropriate formali-ties. Throughout the whole of the local press of this period, 1900—1912, there is not a single case of sickness or accident refused the appropriate medical or hospital service.

The hospitals were then, of course, all under the voluntary system, and were mainly financed by endowments and by the collections which took place every year in almost every town and village throughout the country. The success of the system may be gauged from the fact that Britain during these years led the world (with one exception—New Zealand) in the lowness of the infant mortality rate and the death rate. This is the more astonishing when we realise that the doctors of that day had neither penicillin, " M. and B.", or the hundred other medicines which have been such a tremendous advantage to us during the past decade.

None of these schemes covered dentistry or optical services, but in 1905 school dentists came into operation, and from then onwards there was a free dental service for all elementary school children, and tooth-brushes were sold at 1½d. each so as to encourage proper care of the teeth. School optical services came in a little later, but still there was no alternative for the elderly with decadent teeth or failing eyesight but to go to the specialist of their choice and pay the appropriate fees. Dentists were now becoming reliable, though not yet registered, and at Stony Stratford and Wolverton Messrs. Goddard and Bull attended one day a week. It was about this time that " painless dentistry " came into being, for hitherto in the rural areas, there was little other than straightforward extraction without gas or cocaine to master the aching tooth. In the more remote villages the smith or the barber did yeoman service in this manner, and the approved " deadener " was a tot of whisky (a mere threepennyworth) which was held over the tooth for a time and then swallowed.

In these days every dentist had outside his surgery a little museum case full of the most repellant specimens of false teeth in various settings.

In addition to the Provident Dispensaries most families belonged to the Good Samaritan Society, from which, in return for a penny a week, sick-room utensils of all kinds could be borrowed in case of illness.

THE FRIENDLY SOCIETIES

The Friendly Societies were at this time approaching the zenith of their activities. The history of these societies in our neighbourhood goes back at least 150 years. The oldest in Stony Stratford appears to have started at the Crown Inn, Stony Stratford, on May 10th, 1794, and in the files of the Registrar of Friendly Societies there is an old rule book which begins :

Articles and Rules for the regulation and Government of the Friendly Society held at the house of Mr. Thomas Blabey, known by the sign of the Crown at Stony Stratford, Bucks. Established July 10th, 1794, enrolled at the Quarter Sessions at Aylesbury, November 3rd, 1794. Printed by William Nixon, Bookseller, Stationer, etc., Stony Stratford, 1858.

The Society transferred its activities to the Swan Inn, High Street, sometime before 1870, and it was dissolved in 1880 when it had 37 members.

There was also a Female Friendly Society which was registered in October 1843, but appears to have been established as early as 1803, and was dissolved in 1898 after nearly a century of existence. It had then 39 members, and £1,026 in Consols and cash. The assets were distributed amongst the members.

These Societies (and there were comparable ones in Calverton and "Wolverton"), were in the main small clubs in which the feature of good fellowship was often in the ascendant, and that of assurance for sickness or death an accessory, but where the Wolverton and Calverton Societies disappeared after a few years, the two Stratford ones had a long record of existence. Many of the smaller societies merged into the Manchester Unity Independent Order of Oddfellows, or the Ancient Order of Foresters, and by uniting gained much greater strength. By the end of the nineteenth century, the strongest of all was the Manchester Unity of Oddfellows, which had nearly a million members up and down the country, but it was strongly challenged by the Ancient Order of Foresters, which had about 700,000 members. Smaller societies were the Hearts of Oak, the National Deposit, and of course the Good Samaritans, all of which had an income of about £1,000,000, and paid out most of it in benefits.

Locally these societies were represented at Stony Stratford by the Duke of Buckingham Lodge of the Manchester Unity of Oddfellows, the Court Prosperity of the Ancient Order of Foresters, and the North Bucks Oddfellows Peabody Lodge (National Independent Order of Oddfellows), and at Wolverton by the Loyal Poor Man's Friend Lodge of the M.U.I.O.O.F. and the Hearts of Oak. The oldest of all these local branches was probably the Stantonbury Court of Good Intent, which was quickly followed in 1867 by the North Bucks District Oddfellows, usually known as the Peabodys. But larger than all these was the London and North Western Railway Provident Society, which had a local membership of 3,750 in 1910. The next largest local branch of any Friendly Society was the

National Deposit, which had 800 members. The others mentioned above had memberships of between 330 and 630, so that in the area of Stony Stratford, Wolverton and Stantonbury, no less than 7,861 were members of some Friendly Society or other. It is not too much to say that every working class family was covered in this way.

All of these gathered in subscriptions of a few pence per week, in return for which there was sick-pay when the member fell ill, and payment of hospital fees if hospitalisation was necessary. But all the funds did not come from subscriptions, for public collections were by no means infrequent. Every year there would be a great torchlight procession, usually in October, when all the local friendly societies from the area, accompanied by their banners and the bands from Stony Stratford, Bradwell, Potterspury, Yardley or Newport Pagnell, together with the town fire brigade decorated with chinese lanterns and all its members in fancy dress, would parade around the town and take a collection—which usually came to about £10. Later this sum was devoted to the Whitsun sports.

A word must be said about the banners and regalia. Each and every prosperous branch had its own banner, which was not of the modest size now favoured by the British Legion or the Women's Institute, but a vast affair possibly 10 ft. by 10 ft., and very beautifully designed and decorated. In one of our illustrations can be seen such a banner, and it needs no imagination to conceive how difficult they were to handle in a high wind. Accompanying the banner would be the office holders with sashes and badges. None of these, however, could quite compare with the Freemasons whose personal regalia was then and is now a thing of splendour. In the Craufurd Arms Ballroom there is a delightful portrait of Canon Harnett in Masonic regalia which shows how seriously he took his Masonic duties. Most clergymen at the time belonged to one or the other of these organisations and often attained high office.

Notwithstanding the clerical aid, most of these branches met at public houses. At Stony Stratford for example, the Duke of Buckingham Oddfellows first met at the old Plough, and in the next half century switched to the Cross Keys, the George, and the Crown. The Peabodys met first at the Cross Keys, then at the Plough until 1874, the Prince of Wales until 1891, and at the Bull Hotel from 1891 to about 1914.

It is difficult to describe to-day the wonderful influence of these societies. They were without question kindly and competent societies whose great aim was to help the sick or fallen brother and his family. There was a tremendous atmosphere of Christian helpfulness, and also one of modest pride in their very considerable achievements. Unfortunately there was occasionally, but only very occasionally, a weak or uncertain treasurer, but by and large they were well administered and a remarkable feature of an England that has passed.

SANITATION

Despite the efforts of local doctors and friendly societies the death rate, the infantile mortality rate, and the sickness rate, were all high in the 1870's, but in that year there occurred one case of sickness which was destined to alter the whole sanitary system of England. The Prince of Wales caught typhoid fever, and nearly died ; and the cause was probably rightly diagnosed as impure drinking water due to a faulty sewage system.

By the end of the 1870's improved sanitation became a political battle cry. Disraeli's famous saying : " Sanitas Sanitatum, omnia Sanitas " became the foundation of several Acts of Parliament which made it incumbent upon municipalities to provide a proper water supply. Both in Wolverton and Stony Stratford this had always been a difficulty. When Wolverton was first growing, the Railway Company had great difficulty in locating a pure water supply. For a time canal and well water were used without discrimination, and the Station Doctor (Dr. Corfe) at the time was overwhelmed by the number of cases of skin disease, liver and pulmonary disorders, and even cholera. In the first six months of 1848 more than 100 local cases of this kind were sent to the Middlesex Hospital. Later in the century most Wolverton cases went to Northampton Hospital, but the incidence was still great. Meanwhile the Railway Company sank new wells, and improved the quality of the supply, but the rapid growth of the town always meant that the supply was irregular, and often in the summer months it would fail completely The extension of the modern sewage system at Wolverton and Bradwell in 1900 meant a still greater call on water supplies.

At Stony Stratford the position was even worse. In the older part of the town, that is to say the High Street, the Market

Square and the Green, there were in 1880 still the old wells and pumps some of which had probably been sunk in the days of King John. Even as late as 1930 many houses up London Road still relied on well water. There were of course many who said that there was nothing to beat well water, particularly when the wells were sunk into the local limestone which of itself was a natural filter. But those wells near the churchyards, or cemeteries, or the river were not quite so free from suspicion, and in flood time every well between the Market Square and the bridge was under water. Typhoid broke out in the town on several occasions, finally—or not so finally as it happened, the Water Tower and Pumping Works were built in 1884, and from Calverton Road to the Gas Works there was now a good water supply.

But somehow or other typhoid did not cease. In the 1890's some members of the Woollard family (which has provided for nearly a century a most distinguished array of local councillors) were struck down, and then, in the 1890's, some members of the family of Mr. Wood, the Old Wolverton miller, were afflicted. Mr. Wood promptly claimed expenses and damages from the Council, and got them.

All this helped one of our local doctors, " Paddy " Maguire, who first came here in 1872, in his campaign for a proper sewage system ; up to this period very few of our local houses had an inside privy. " The necessary house " as the lawyers still called it, was still built separately from the house, often alongside the coal shed, and the visit to one or the other in the cold winter mornings was anything but a pleasure. The needs of the night, or of the sick, were met by the universal provision of a " chamber " under the bed, or in the more wealthy dwellings, of a " night commode ", often quite a beautiful piece of furniture, and which has now become the favourite of those who love antique furniture in these days. " Emptying the slops " was of course a daily routine, and the enamelled bucket, complete with lid, was one of the articles often in demand at the local ironmongers.

In addition to emptying the slops, there was the weekly or monthly task of emptying the " sanitary bucket " into a hole dug in the garden, with its inevitable enrichment of the soil, but also with its inevitable smells. For those who had no gardens a " night soil cart," rather like the ancient tumbril, made its not infrequent rounds.

Early in the 1900's events began to move. The Woollards, Maguires, Woods and many others formed a strong phalanx for the installation of a proper sewage system. There were others, who had never had typhoid or cholera, or even a skin disease, who were appalled at the probable cost. £10,000 was mentioned, and this for a small town of less than 3,000 people. The local Council dithered. Finally in June 1903 the Overseers of Stratford called a special meeting at the Public Hall so as to test public opinion, and Mr. S. R. Rooke, Chairman for many years of the Stony Stratford Parish Council, was voted to the Chair. According to the report in the *North Bucks Advertiser* for June 19th, 1903, Mr. F. W. Woollard, C.C., opened the proceedings by explaining that the then limited sewage system had four outlets, one across the meadows to Calverton, one below the Stony Stratford Mill, one near the Gas House, and one near Old Wolverton Mill. The two mill outlets had a trick of getting blocked up from time to time, and the sewage missed the settling beds and went direct into the river. This inadequate system, installed in 1883, after an outbreak of typhoid in the town, was certainly no longer efficient, and an infinitely better system was required, and this would probably cost £15,000, whereas the entire rateable value of the town was only £6,000. Buckingham and Stantonbury had recently installed sewerage schemes and the cost was great.

Mr. J. S. Tibbetts followed, and pointed out that the money would have to be borrowed, and this needed the approval of the Local Government Board. A general discussion followed, then Mr. W. J. Markham caught the Chairman's eye and asked : " Whether Mr. Woollard and Mr. Tibbetts were in favour of doing away with one of the worst curses to a working man's house in Stony Stratford, namely the sanitary bucket ? " Mr. Tibbetts replied at once that he too thought the bucket system the curse of the town, and that was why the whole question of the sewerage scheme had been brought up. " A greater nuisance could not exist than those buckets ".

Mr. J. Elmes then put the other side. Nobody, he said, wanted an elaborate scheme, and the cost of a large scheme to the ratepayers would be very heavy. If it were to be a large and expensive scheme he would certainly oppose it. Eventually it was resolved that the Chairman write to the District Council asking if they would receive a deputation urging that there should be an efficient sewage scheme, but not too expensive please !

The District Council fortified by this strong expression of opinion took the appropriate action, and in May 1905 the contract was signed and sealed. But the eventual cost was neither £10,000 nor £15,000, it was £17,000 plus an additional £3,000 for new roads (York and Augustus Roads) and other houses built soon after the contract was drawn up.

For a year or so the town was in an upheaval, and it is interesting but unsatisfactory to record that when the deep trench for the sewage pipes was being dug near the Gas Works, walls over a yard thick of an old building were discovered. But nobody was interested, and even the exact location was unrecorded by engineer or clerk. It is possible that such a stout masonry building might have been the ruins of the long forgotten Chapel or Hospital of St. John which used to stand by the causeway to the bridge from 1240 to 1380.

About the same period, August 1906, the new sewerage works were completed at Wolverton, and for the first time in history Wolverton, Stony Stratford, and Stantonbury all had fairly adequate sanitation. Yet inspite of all this, there were still 126 cesspools in the Wolverton area which had to be emptied by the Sanitary authority. The sludge cart was still in use !

It is perhaps no small wonder that the introduction of adequate sewage schemes, and tapped water supplies should have had such a great effect on public health, and during the decade under review infantile mortality in this locality dropped by nearly half, and the death rate was considerably reduced. In all these vital statistics this area showed up better than most parts of England and Wales, though it always lagged behind Hertfordshire, Dorsetshire, and Wilts.

But there was another great advantage, for piped water and sanitary closets were but the first of the labour saving devices that were to lighten so much the daily work of women. Pumping and carrying water, emptying the slops, and so on were greatly minimised.

FIRES

From time to time in the local press we strike the note of disaster that comes from a distressing fire. There were few living in Wolverton at this time who could not remember the fire of November 25, 1882, when Wolverton Works suffered one of its most fearful devastations. It started in the body-shop, spread almost to the sawmill, and within a few hours had completely gutted about half of the Works. So complete was the damage that everybody was " stood off ", and for some weeks there was very little to spend in Wolverton. Soon after the L.N.W.Ry. introduced a new fire engine, and housed it in the newly built fire station just opposite the Royal Engineer, and it was linked by the newly introduced telegraph with all places along the main G.P.O. routes and railway lines. But in spite of these improvements, and the telegraph, the Wolverton Fire Brigade was often late on the scene compared with the Stony Stratford Fire Brigade. The latter then had as its Captain, George Downing, who was one of the most efficient Captains this area has ever known, and he himself worked at his black-smith's shop at the corner of the London Road and the Green. He knew not only every trick and turn in the roads hereabouts, but also the location of every pond, brook, or drain that would provide water ; in addition to this, he knew where and when the fastest cyclists of Stratford were to be found, and as each of these knew every member of the Fire Brigade, the call out was swift. Moreover, the Stratford brigade could use post horses, whilst Wolverton had light cart horses. Thus, when a disastrous fire broke out at Castlethorpe on August 4, 1906, and a dozen thatched houses were soon a blazing inferno, the distracted in-habitants immediately telegraphed for the Wolverton Fire Brigade, and sent off a cyclist for the Stratford Brigade. The cyclist (as the *Wolverton Express* records without comment) was delayed en route, but nevertheless the Stony Stratford Brigade arrived first on the scene.

The actual fire was the second of its kind in Castlethorpe within six years, but this was the more severe. It started in Back Street, when the thatched roof of a stable was set on fire by—it was thought—a spark from a passing train. There was a high wind, and soon the flames were leaping high, and portions of burning thatch were carried all over the place. The nearby Lack's Yard and Varney's Yard were missed, mainly owing to their slate roofs, but, soaring over these, the blazing torchlets set alight still more thatched houses in Fleet Street. All that both fire bridages could do was to limit the area of destruction, which they did very successfully just before the local water supplies completely gave out. Meanwhile, the news reached the Works ; immediately the management gave the order that all Castlethorpe men were to get to the Station. The very next express train was stopped, in clambered the men, on the express train roared until Castlethorpe, when the men all helped in the melancholy task of trying to save a little of what was left, and of fixing up accommodation for the 38 displaced parishioners in the local school, railway station, etc.

There were, as always, some curious stories circulating after the fire, but the two which were certainly true were that one of the families, the Pells, had had the misfortune to be burnt out twice in six years, whilst another labourer, Mr. Clarke, recovered £20 in gold from his own house by sifting the ashes.

A Relief Committee was quickly formed, and over £100 subscribed—which seems little enough now, but when we remember that a complete house could then be furnished for £15, it went a long way to make good some of the losses of the unfortunate people, though it by no means compensated the house owners, the principal of whom was Lord Carrington.

Whilst we are on the subject of Castlethorpe, it is interesting to add that the same issue of the *Wolverton Express* which gives the details of the fire also records that the age-old " Tom and Jerry " Public House had ceased to exist, and that its licence had been transferred to the newly established " Carrington Arms ".

In September 1906 there was a fire at the Wolverton Market Hall which was then near the steam Laundry of the L.N.W.Ry. and Glynn Square. Over £1,000 worth of damage was done, and for several weeks afterwards the market was held in the open air. Subsequently the market was installed in the old Schools at the corner of Creed Street, where it still takes place on the traditional Fridays.

GOLD

Perhaps the most extraordinary local story of the amount of gold and silver that ordinary people kept in their houses comes from Bletchley. Round about the years 1882—1900 a family named Payne lived at 35, Bletchley Road. There was nothing to indicate that they were either richer or poorer than most of their neighbours. In the ensuing years there were several changes of tenants, and the Bletchley Co-op bought the house in 1911. In 1925 Mr. W. J. Hing, grocery manager of the Bletch-

Photograph lent by Miss Maguire

OLD STRATFORD CROSS ROADS IN THE 1900'S

The old Watling Street at Old Stratford was then barely wide enough for two carts at a time, consequently with the coming of motor traffic it became imperative to widen this bottle neck.　The house on the right was Mr. Judge's wheelrights shop, whilst on the left may be seen a row of cottages and the Falcon Inn, all of which were pulled down in the 1920's to permit the widening of the corners.　See p. 113.

Photograph lent by Mr. H. Swain

THE WOLVERTON CENTRAL CLUB IN 1907.

The Club had only just been opened.　In the background may be seen the newly erected houses in Western Road.　The walled enclosure contains the quoit beds of the club and the small lawn, both of which have now been built over.　The band is that of the Wolverton Companies of the Bucks Volunteers.　See p. 115.

Photograph by Thorneycroft

PASSENHAM TITHE BARN

This remarkable barn was built partly about 1500 and partly in 1626, and is said to have housed some of Cromwell's troops during the Civil War. In the 1900's Passenham Manor and the Tithe Barn belonged to the Countess of Warwick, a great friend of King Edward VII. See p. 41.

ley Co-op, began to live there. In 1941, it was decided to put a new water supply pipe in, and this meant taking up tiles in the pantry. To the astonishment of " plain Charles Dickens " who was doing some of the work, he unearthed a rusty tin box under the tiles. It was found to contain £310 in gold, about £40 in silver, a 15-carat gold chain, and a silver watch inscribed " G. F. Payne, Bedford, 1862 ". Strenuous efforts were made to find the legal owners of this treasure trove, without result, and finally a Coroner's Court (Mr. E. T. Ray) formally seized the treasure on behalf of the Crown, and Mr. Dickens, the finder was rewarded by receiving about 75 per cent. of the value of the find.

Just one further story to cap this. When the old White Swan was being reconstructed at Stony Stratford, the workmen came across a jar full of gold coins—all Roman—and unquestionably of great value. Nothing was said at the time, but one of the workmen subsequently became very prosperous. A year ago the sole survivor of the party showed me the last gold coin he had kept. It was a beauty—as large as a florin, and as clear as when it was minted.

CHAPTER VIII

Sports and Pastimes

LOOKING BACK OVER half a century there would not appear to have been much change in the English way of spending leisure time as far as sports are concerned. Football is still the king of winter sports, and cricket undoubtedly the king of summer sports or games, whilst hockey, rugger, swimming and angling still have their many devotees.

But a deeper glance reveals that there has been a most definite change in what we might call the minor sports. Quoits, which used to be played behind the taverns and clubs of almost every town and village has almost passed out. No longer do we hear the ring of wrought steel on steel as quoit clips quoit in the clayey bed. One of the best quoit " beds " in Stratford used to be behind the Old White Hart Inn on the Market Square, which was kept up for many years by the Workmen's Club when it was in those premises. It was a rare pitch in a walled-in enclosure specially arranged for the purpose, and with a covered loggia along the one side where drinks would be served to players and watchers.

Another delightful set of beds were to be found behind the Prince of Wales Inn, along the Wolverton Road, where from February 1901 the newly-formed Stony Stratford Quoits Club had its headquarters. The best team in the district, however, came from Stantonbury, where at the Social Club there was a pitch which from 1906 onwards was the cradle of many first class players.

For years Stantonbury was champion of the local Quoits League, and up to 1907 were unbeatable.

But gradually Wolverton Social Club players began to improve, and great was the jubilation when in 1907 the famous Stantonbury team were defeated. For several years Wolverton continued to improve and up to the outbreak of the first world War were in their turn unbeatable. In one year, 1909, with the help of Joe Smith, a really great player, they won the League without losing a single game.

Quoits, however, suffered from two disadvantages, it was a dirty game in the sense that the clay on the quoits made one's hands filthy ; and moreover it was not a game which could be reported with any great skill in the local press.

Yet oddly enough, it was replaced by bowls, a game which after having been illegal for centuries, gradually infiltrated into the district from about 1890 onwards. It is interesting to recall that for centuries every apprentice in the area on taking up his apprenticeship had to sign an indenture on which he faithfully promised not to frequent Taverns or Ale Houses, nor to play at " Dice, Cards, Tables (skittles), Bowls, or other unlawful games ". It was not until about 1845 that these stringent regulations were relaxed.

The first bowling green in the neighbourhood appears to have been at Wolverton Park, which from 1890 onwards had a green and teams of great merit. Stony Stratford apparently had no bowls green until 1923, when the Bowls section of the Sports Club was started.

It was the same with tennis, or rather lawn tennis, which again first came into vogue at Wolverton in the 1890's at the Park. The first report of any match in the *Wolverton Express* is in June 1905, when Wolverton Park played a Stantonbury team. Gradually the popularity of the game increased ; it became an asset to almost every vicarage in the neighbourhood ; and tea on the Rectory lawn, in the shade of great elms or yew trees, with a tennis court or croquet lawn in the immediate vicinity made a picture so English as to be commemorated by many notable artists.

But for the really hot days of the summer few pastimes were equal to bathing or boating. Then, as now, the need for good bathing places at Stratford and Wolverton was a perennial matter for discussion, but the local lads never waited on their elders, and favourite spots were the Mill pools, " The Poplars," near Passenham, the Barley Mow, at Stratford, and the Viaduct at Wolverton. Unfortunately there was a steady toll of deaths through swimming in these or other unauthorised places, and in fact there was no place nearer than Newport where swimming could be considered safe.

Boating, too, was popular with the young and grown-ups alike. In the early part of the century there were half a dozen thatched boathouses along the Mill Race at Stony Stratford, whilst on the canal side at Wolverton there was the flourishing

Livonia Boating Club, which had over a hundred members. One of the prettiest sights of the summer was to see the boats and canoes of all shapes and sizes along the Canal between Cosgrove and Bradwell. The Livonia Boating Club used to have its annual regatta and sports, and organised many visits by canal to neighbouring villages or towns.

Angling, too, had its devotees, for in those days the Ouse between Buckingham and Newport was a pure limpid stream alive with fish, and the canal from Buckingham to Cosgrove was one of the pleasantest fishing waters in the country. Angling rights were strongly held. The Deanshanger and Old Stratford Angling Association held most of the rights along the canal ; whilst the Wolverton and Stantonbury Fishing Association covered most of the rights in that neighbourhood, including the Back Water near the Iron Trunk. There were some remarkably fine catches of perch, dace, pike, and other freshwater fish.

FOOTBALL

Football then, as now, was the most popular sport, and every Thursday and Saturday would see every football pitch in the neighbourhood occupied. Every village ran a team or two, whilst the towns had as many as half a dozen under all sorts of designations. Churches, chapels, schools, firms, and clubs, all had their teams, and in the main friendly matches were played.

On top of all these were two local leagues, and two cup competitions in which the rivalry was traditional. These were the Buckingham League, the Ascott League, and the Berks and Bucks Junior and Minor Cups. Within the decade the leagues were to reach their peak of popularity, and fade and die, never to be resuscitated in quite the same form.

There was great local jubilation when in 1900 the Stantonbury St. James' team, which had been the winners of the Buckingham League for three years in succession, also won the Berks and Bucks Cup. It was the first time this cup had ever been won by a team from the north of the county.

The Buckingham League was founded in 1897, and its moving spirit throughout the next decade was Mr. H. E. Bull, J.P., of Castle House, Buckingham. Teams from miles around took part, and for the winning team at the end of the year there was a splendid silver cup, and a medal for each player. It was the same with the Ascott League, and the Berks and Bucks Cups, which, however, included teams a little further south. Only once in the history of these clubs did a single team win three of these honours, and that was Stony Stratford early in the century.

In those days the Stony Stratford Football Club had its head-quarters at the Prince of Wales Inn (now No. 68, Wolverton Road), and the pitch was in a four-acre field owned by Mr. J. S. Tibbetts behind the Inn. The Inn had a backway to the field, and a most profitable temporary bar on the field boundary. Mr. J. S. Tibbetts was the President for many years, Mr. W. J. Markham, the Secretary, Mr. S. McBright, the Treasurer, and amongst the players were Jimmy Hull, the Captain, Stanley Woollard, the speedy outside right, Bob Rickson, as centre, and the two Cockerills in the forward line. In 1907-8 they won the Buckingham and the Ascott Leagues—the former with only ten men against Wolverton in the final game. Local jubilation can be imagined—there were the processions around the town, with Jimmy Hull carried shoulder-high waving the cup which streamed with beer and the green and black ribbons of the Club.

This team was the last to play on the Prince of Wales ground, for the field was sold to Mr. Franklin in 1907 and a year later Clarence Road was planned and building had started.

It is a sad story, but in many ways an exciting one, which re-cords the partial decline of local league football in this area between 1909 and 1919, for up to the former date public interest not unnaturally centred upon the League matches—that is to say, the Buckingham League and the Ascott League. In all of these Wolverton and Stony Stratford met, every year for a decade, and were usually both very near the top. As can be imagined the local " Derby " produced great crowds and intense excitement ; but perhaps the medal for excitement (or rather the blackest of black marks) should go to a match played in the Buckingham League at Newport Pagnell in April 1907. Newport Pagnell and Fenny Stratford Rovers met on the Woad Farm ground at Newport. After twenty minutes of play, F. Kilsby, one of the Fenny forwards, ran through to shoot, but the ball was caught by the Newport goalie. Kilsby charged him, and had the surprise of his life when the Newport goalie kicked him back. The Referee, Mr. R. Williams, of Wolverton, promptly ordered the goalie off the field. The rest of the game was unmelodious in the extreme. Fenny won 2—1 against the depleted Newport side, and as the final whistle went the crowd made a dash, not only for the referee, which would have been in keeping with local tradition, but for the Fenny forwards, and two of them, Kilsby and F. Vince, were caught, and pushed into the river. The crowd then made its way to the Ram Hotel, where the Fenny team were changing, and when, after an interval, the Rovers came out and tried to go home in their brake, they were met with a shower of stones, rotten eggs, fish, and garbage. Two cycles were smashed in the melee, and the driver of the brake and several players injured.

I asked one of those who took part in this scene where the rotten eggs had come from : the answer came " My uncle had a sitting hen behind the Neptune Inn ! "

Meanwhile the Police had arrived, and in some way managed to restore order, after taking the names of the leading culprits. The brake then left for Fenny. But the crowd were by no means satisfied as yet, for they took a short cut and caught up with the brake along the Willen Road, near what was then and is still, Cowley's Parchment Works, where the river comes out in a shallow bend then often used for the washing down of carriages. A determined effort was made to upset the brake into the water, but the Fenny team gave as good as they got, and finally arrived home with several casualties.

Such behaviour called for action. The first repercussion was at the Newport Petty Sessions the next Wednesday, when the three ringleaders were each fined 2s. 6d. and costs, or seven days. It was, of course, said that if they had been tried at Fenny they would all have been jailed for life !

The next repercussion was more serious. The League officials held an enquiry ; Newport Town Football Club received a stern admonition and was heavily fined. The Club could not, or more probably would not, pay ; consequently it disappeared, and for many years Newport Town was not on the football map.

Fortunately such incidents were rare, and by and large football was played as it should have been played, but the incident was enough to put the first large nail into the temporary coffin of local league football.

The second came in 1907, when Wolverton under the leadership of Mr. W. Knight, with Mr. W. Gee, as Secretary and Mr. R. Noble as Treasurer, decided to withdraw from the Buckinghamshire leagues and to enter the Northampton League. In the following years other teams dropped out for several reasons, and Mr. H. E. Bull resigned the Presidency of the Buckingham

League in September 1909. For the Ascott League only two teams entered that year.

There was one other factor that helped to destroy local football. The Football Association had recently created the Southern League, and Northampton Town was one of the aspirants for the Championship. Its unexpected success brought crowds of spectators from this locality to the Cobblers' ground at Northampton.

Yet although local league football was dead, the smaller teams carried on with gusto. Both at Wolverton and Stony Stratford there were half a dozen teams in full run in 1910, apart from the various schoolboy football teams.

To the younger generation in Stony Stratford in the 1900's no football was keener than that which was played for the Schools' Football Cup, from 1903 onwards. There were then four elementary boys schools in the town, the two church schools of St. Giles and St. Mary's, the non-conformist school, or British School, and the school for the Orphanage boys.

In 1904 and 1905 St. Giles, which was the largest school, won the cup. The next year St. Mary's and St. Giles met in the final in Downing's Field. The match was a draw 3—3, a very remarkable achievement on the part of St. Mary's who were three down at half-time. The replay resulted in a victory by 3—0 for St. Mary's. It is difficult now even to describe the jubilation that followed. The victors were carried shoulder-high around the town to the strains of the Town Band, and to the St. Mary's schoolboys at the time, the sight of the cup streaming with blue and white ribbons was almost the greatest thrill of their young lives. The teams were:

St. Mary's :
Butcher
Green Pratt
A. Smith Ross Shirley
Downing Biddle Jelley Pratt J. Smith
o

St. Giles :
Meacham Morris Westley Canvin Roberts
Goodridge Johnson Pattison
Millward Harrison
Sprittles

One of the saddest commentaries of our times is that nearly half of these young players were killed in the first World War.

Cricket, though less exciting in one sense, had its crowds of devotees throughout the summer, and among the better Wolverton players of the period may be noted W. J. Brown, D. Mackey, and S. F. Lawman as batsmen, whilst amongst the bowlers were G. Goodman, P. Woolliams and D. Mackey. Mackey was indeed an all-round sportsman, for we also find him prominent in hockey and football matches. In 1907 no less than four members of the Wolverton hockey team had played for the County—T. Tibbetts, T. C. Boulter, H. H. Coker, and A. A. H. Cadwallader.

CYCLING

For many years cycling had been one of the favourite pastime of the youth of Wolverton, and the development was encouraged by the churches or local political bodies. Early in the century there were four outstanding cycling clubs in the town. The Mazeppa, founded in 1892 had over 150 members, and its yearly activities included several paper chases, a hill-climbing competition, free-wheeling competition, parades, cricket matches and an annual dinner. The Reform Cycling Club, founded in 1900, was a Liberal organisation and had as its second function propaganda work for that party. The Constitutional Club was the Conservative reply. The smallest club was the Onyx. These clubs organised an annual cycle parade at which collections were made to support the Wolverton and Bradwell Good Samaritan Society. These annual parades were one of the great events of the year. Every cycle and rider was decorated or adorned in the most ingenious manner, and the gathering place, the Market Square, would be absolutely crowded to see the turnouts of the Mazeppa, Reform, or Constitutional Cycling Clubs, each of which adopted a colourful theme in the hope of winning the challenge cups and prizes of the year. In 1905, for example, the Reform members appeared in oriental costumes in the club colours, with turbans and large yellow sashes. The Mazeppa turned out as Red Indians in all the glory of war-paint and tomahawks. One member had most cleverly constructed a wigwam over and around his cycle (Mr. C. B. Johnson, who thus won the Gents' prize). The Reform won the Cup, and the Mazeppa was second. In addition to these teams competitions, there were the individual prizes for the most comic, most beautiful, or most topical turnout, and the ingenuity that was displayed was fascinating. For several years Miss Lily Elliott won the Ladies Cup. In 1905 she won it as Shamrock, and in 1906 as The Belle of New York. The adjudication was followed by a parade, with the band, of course, all round the town, and then on to the Bradwell Recreation Ground, where the prizes would be presented.

THE HUNTS

Of all the sports and pastimes of this period possibly the most distinguished was the hunt. For eight centuries this part of the world, and particularly southern Northants, had been a royal hunting ground. From Stony Stratford the later Norman kings had gone forth to hunt in Whittlewood Forest, and in Plantagenet times Grafton Regis had seen many royal parties.

Fox-hunting still survived, and in this locality there were the Grafton Hunt and the Whaddon Chase Hunt. Up to 1906 the Master of the Grafton was the Hon. S. E. Douglas Pennant, who in that year was followed by the autocratic Lord Southampton, who was his own huntsman. From time to time the local farmers complained that the Grafton hunted foxes but never killed them, and there was considerable discussion when the Hunt had a meet indoors instead of out. But there was one kill, at least, which was talked about for years. On September 29th, 1906, a fox was turned out of the coverts near Gayhurst House, the residence of Mr. W. W. Carlile, who had recently represented the area in Parliament. The fox dashed for the house, straight across the lawns, and jumped into the dining-room through the open window. The hounds all followed, and the fox was killed on the carpet.

The *Wolverton Express* adds that " no damage was done ", but the maids must have had quite a job cleaning up the mess. For the next few years the Grafton killed about 70 brace of foxes yearly, and the farmers beamed again on the hunt.

Members of the hunt were, of course, quite convinced that by hunting they were rendering great services to the nation ; it encouraged the breeding of good horses, which as everyone knew were a great national asset ; it kept down foxes, though there were some who murmured that the fox would have been extinct long ago but for its preservation for hunting ; but perhaps the limit that could be said in praise of hunting was reached in December 1908 when at the Fat Stock Show Dinner at the Cock Hotel, Stony Stratford, a local M.F.H. state that "unemployment would increase by sixty to seventy per cent. if hunting were done away with ".

The Whaddon Chase, always coupled with the names of the

Selby-Lowndes family, was an exciting hunt, and excitement probably reached its climax in the 1920's when the hunt split into two and argued as much as they chased. A temporary period of peace however was achieved in 1921 when both the Prince of Wales and the Duke of York (now King George VI) joined the hunts at a meet at Great Horwood and had a good day.

Children's sports and pastimes were then very much the same as they are now, but with the exception that two games which required good and fairly empty pavements seem to have almost disappeared. Hoops and tops were very much the vogue every spring in the 1900's. Most of the hoops were made of iron, and some had an iron handle too, but smaller girls enjoyed rolling the wooden hoops. Whips and tops were grand fun, and it seems a pity that these games have been almost forced out of existence with the rapid growth and speed of road transport.

For children especially, some of the great events of the year were the local fairs.

SHOWS AND FAIRS

In an age when the cinema was as yet unthought of, and radio still in its infancy, the local visiting fairs were occasions long looked forward to and greatly enjoyed.

One of the largest fairs that ever visited the locality was that of Barker and Thurstons, who for three days " in Mr. Norman's meadow at Corner Pin, Wolverton " presented a wonderful series of amusements—but perhaps we had better just quote from the actual advertisements in the *Wolverton Express* of August 21st, 1903 :

Barker and Thurston's Grand Carnival
including
The Gilded Gondolas
and
The Original Royal Show of Living Pictures
with its
Gigantic Collection of Costly Reproductions of Life
including
The Great Fantastical TRIP TO THE MOON
In its natural colours
With other Attractive Amusements Making the
GREATEST CARNIVAL EVER HELD

At Stony Stratford the Annual Statute Fair was always held in August, in those days it stretched from the Market Square, along Silver Street, and around the Green. It was now the scene of the first " animated pictures " to be seen in the neighbourhood. Every year Taylor's Bioscope with its monster multi-coloured organ and blazing electric lights vied with Billings' Roundabouts and Thurston's Switchbacks for the public fancy, but these were only the centre pieces of the fair, for all around were not only the traditional coconut shies and rifle stalls, but brandy snap stalls, and stalls where they sold tubes of water for squibbing down girls' necks (a peculiar way of showing one's interest or affection, but always greeted with laughing shrieks). The whole Square would be lit up by naphtha lamps the smell of which was one of the most peculiar and unforgettable things of the fair.

Wolverton probably showed the first indoor animated pictures for from about 1901 onwards Jury and Co's Bioscope was a feature of the annual entertainment given by the Working Men's Club to the children of the town. In 1906, over 600 children were invited, and on leaving were presented with three new pennies (wealth indeed in those days, when a farthing would buy a sugar mouse, or a stick of spanish, or a bag of sweets), two oranges, and a cake of chocolate. The Bioscope was received rapturously, and the programme in 1907 included no less than nine different films—for each film was then only a reel in length, and lasted less than ten or eleven minutes. Here is the list of films then shown :

An Arabian Magician (a trick film this).
Smugglers Dogs.
A Little New Brother (a pathetic story about a starving child, with
     a happy ending).
A Race for a Husband.
The Servant Girl Problem (a farce).
Barcelona Park.
Cabby by the Hour.
A Tenant's Revenge.
The Royal Spanish Wedding (News reel).

The culminating point was possibly reached when, in the middle of the films, the slide showing the features of Mr. Gamble, Secretary to the Games Committee, appeared on the screen. How the children yelled their approval !

These, of course, were the days of the silent screen, but lack of talkie apparatus was often made up for by other means. At

Taylor's Bioscope in Stony Stratford a man sat behind the screen, and whenever he could sing the appropriate song, or make the appropriate noise he did so.

From time to time these fairs were supplemented by the travelling " penny gaffs ", or travelling theatres, which usually presented a programme of lurid melodrama in which the villain really was a villain, and the heroine usually in tears over her " chee-ild ". In April 1907, for example, the Victoria Theatre set up in the Newport Road, Stantonbury, and its plays varied from " The Sacred Trust " to " Wine and Women ". It is interesting to note that the advertisements claimed that the theatre was " free from vulgarity ".

FLOWER SHOWS

The local flower shows were also enjoyed with gusto. Every year there would be great shows at Wakefield Lodge, Lathbury Park, Wolverton Park, Tickford Abbey Park, and so on, with thousands of entries and thousands of spectators. These flower shows were often the scenes of intense rivalry as to who could produce the best carrots, or roses, or the best baked cakes. Usually two or more great marquees were erected in the Park, or a local field, and soon filled with the nostalgic aroma of roses and carnations or with the earthier smell of potatoes, celery and just plain pungent onions. All this, mixed with the smell of canvas and perspiration made an assault on the nostril unforgettable and unforgotten. The local band would, of course, be there, and often side shows and roundabouts, and the day would finish off with dancing on the lawn in the evening.

As the years went on these flower shows became more and more ambitious. Each tried to give the greatest number of prizes and to get the greatest number of entries and visitors. Just before the first world war, in 1909, the Stony Stratford Annual Flower Show Society was formed with W. J. Elmes, as its president, Art R. Elmes, as Hon. Treasurer, and W. J. Markham, as Hon. Secretary, and to the Flower Show they added a colourful military tournament by famous cavalry regiments.

Possibly the greatest attendances were secured by the Flower Show at Lathbury Park, then in the occupation of William Trevor. The stone and tile mansion was built in 1790, and there is a lovely park with a fine lawn. It was here that many flower shows and other fetes were held for well over a century. Our illustration shows such a flower show in the year 1900. The three large marquees can be seen, together with Billing's roundabouts, Thurston's switchbacks and all the fun of the fair. Over 2,000 people visited this particular gathering, and as our illustration shows they all appear to be well-dressed in the fashions of the time, but all very serious at such an important ceremony as having a photograph taken.

Unfortunately there was one side to these flower shows that reflects sadly and badly upon our locality. It will readily be imagined that local rivalry on these occasions was intense, for there was much local honour and glory in sweeping off a series of First Prizes at these shows. There were instances when a formidable competitor in the onion class, for example, found that his best onions had been " lifted " a few evenings before the show. But the pilfering did not stop there, and at the Stony Stratford Flower Show in 1912 there were several despicable thefts which caused considerable annoyance. One exhibitor lost a plate of tomatoes, another a dish of peas, and a third was unable to trace a collection of apples, and it was shrewdly suspected that these had been stolen by an exhibitor who was preparing for another show. But the worst case of all was the theft of four yards of beautiful pillow lace made by an old widow lady, Mrs. Savage, of Beachampton, which was even then valued at 5/- a yard. The police were, of course, called in, but it was too late to discover the culprits.

One odd result of this sort of thing was that one of the finest gardeners in the locality, Mr. " Jimmy " French, who had an isolated garden adjoining the pumping station along the Calverton Road, used to keep a night long watch over his produce just before any show in which he was exhibiting.

Unquestionably the Flower Shows were really one of the features of the time, but they were not quite the perfect examples of brotherly trust and respect that we should like to think them.

SPORTS

One of the greatest events of the year was the Wolverton Amateur Athletic Whitsun Sports, which were held in the Park. For a period of about thirty years the Whitsun Festival was regarded in Wolverton and Stantonbury as a time for family reunion and sporting jollification. The Park itself was an almost ideal ground for the cycle races, flat races, and so on, which attracted competitors from all over the country, and the Park would attract well over 2,000 persons during the two days of the sports.

In addition to this, there were the balls on both nights, held in one of the large railway workshops, which, of course, was specially arranged and decorated for the purpose. In the centre would be erected a bandstand, which was usually occupied by the Wednesbury Prize Band. From 8 o'clock each evening everybody—or nearly everybody—danced the old-time dances with gusto.

These festivities would be preceded by a luncheon at the Science and Art Institute, which was really a re-union of Old Wolvertonians—a term which then belonged to the Institute and not to the Grammar School.

Stratford, of course, had little say in these festivities, so it arranged its own. The Whitsun Annual Sports there usually held in Malletts Close, were arranged by the Friendly Societies, and were not unnaturally preceded by a procession all around the town in which the banners of the Societies were carried high to the tunes of the Stony Stratford Prize Band.

Of all the processions none could equal those arranged early in the century by a curious organisation calling itself " The Darktown Charity Organisation ". It was a most remarkable combination of a nigger minstrel troupe, decorated carts, clowns, a tin kettle band, giants and regal equestrians. In the summer of 1900 this organisation arranged four distinct carnivals—at Wolverton, Stony Stratford, Newport Pagnell and Stantonbury, the purpose of which was to collect money for the benefit of " those called to South Africa and their dependents within six miles of Wolverton ". At each of the four places the procession would start from some central point and then parade all around the town with dancing, singing, clowning and general bustling all helping to increase the general merriment. Often there would be a torchlight procession at the conclusion. Over £100 was collected by these four carnivals.

Remarkable ingenuity was displayed in the decoration of the carts, and it is difficult to find out which was the more impressive but there does appear to be a distinct leaning towards one which bore " His Satanic Majesty and Four Imps". One of our photographs shows the Stantonbury Carnival commencing. The Bradwell Nigger Minstrel Troupe can be seen in the foreground ; on the right is Mr. Eady of Wolverton in dashing attire on a tired horse. At the moment of the photograph all the jollity had stopped, for in those days having a photograph taken was quite a serious business, and everybody stood stock still whilst the man under the dark cloth made the dicky bird fly out. But in a couple of minutes the festivity was resumed with vigour.

THE BANDS

One of the most remarkable features of life in father's day was the almost universal pleasure everybody got from the local bands. From the smallest villages to the largest towns, everybody loved a band, and there were few entertainments or public occasions that could be considered complete without at least one band. One of the more important occasions, as for example the torchlight processions usually held in October, there were four bands, and if the procession were a long one (and they mostly were) two or more bands would be playing at once.

Naturally with such a wealth of players, there would be the most acute differences in technique, not infrequently accentuated by the frequency with which people would offer drinks to the Band, but usually the big drum managed to swallow up every discordant sound. In some villages band practices were almost a village re-union. At Great Horwood the bandmaster, Mr. Elmes (cousin of the Elmes at Stony Stratford), was also the village smith, and in consequence band practices were held in the smithy, where the youth of the village would congregate, since there was nowhere else save the " pubs ".

In 1894, after somewhat of a bad spell, the Stony Stratford Band was re-organised, and in 1906 succeeded in securing silver instruments, then the aim and ambition of every band. It was this band which caused considerable public discussion in 1911 on the occasion of King George V's coronation. The Coronation Committee offered to pay the band 7/6 per man in addition to a free tea, but the band felt that 10/- was the least they expected, and for a week or two the tension was absurd. Finally, in a truly British spirit, a compromise was made and King George duly honoured by the loyal strains of the Silver band.

MUSIC IN THE AIR

It was not only the bands which supplied the music of the period, for there was still the Victorian love of the piano, and the newer love for that dreadful instrument the early phono-graph.

I think that at this period every other house had a piano ; in fact no working man's home was considered complete without one. They cost from £20 upwards, and were, of course, always located in the parlour. To be able to play the piano was no small social accomplishment, and nearly always at Christmas the family groups would gather around and sing the age old carols in no uncertain voices. Music mistresses abounded, and found an ample supply of pupils of all ages.

But the piano was not the only home instrument ; many houses invested in a harmonium, and in many others the playing of the violin, the concertina, or the piccolo, was a regular Sunday evening delight.

The concertina had a vogue of its own, rather like that which the accordion has to-day, and it seemed to have been created either for the more solemn forms of church music, or the silliest of silly songs. Sillier than all was the new phonograph. Edison had marketed this dreadful instrument of torture in 1888, and by 1895 the early models were to be found in a few public houses locally and a few years later almost everywhere. What-ever the theme the record always began in a nasal voice with " Edison Bell Record " and finished with the same twanging sign-off. Most of the records too, seem to have been made by untrained singers from Kansas or Chicago, and since the instru-ment itself was far from being mechanically perfect the resultant raucous din was enough to frighten any child or dog.

However, whatever the instrument, there were few families who could not produce reasonably good music when required, and indeed in many instances the combination of good piano playing, a good violin, and sweet voices gave one the same thrill that Pepys had when he listened to good chamber music.

Sweeter than the raucous phonograph were the barrel organs. Barely a day went by without an itinerant organ-grinder, some-times with a monkey, seeking coppers from all and sundry whilst he ground out the popular tunes of the day.

INNS AND TAVERNS

Of all local pastimes the most time-honoured was the visit to the local, and certainly from time immemorial Stony Strat-ford, and villages such as Loughton, had never lacked a variety of choice for those who liked the flowing ale and the flowing

High Street
& Inns
1900

STONY STRATFORD HIGH STREET AND INNS IN 1900

Drawn by C. W. Green

The Town centre of the fifteenth century was hereabouts, and many of the ancient Inns are existing although converted to shops and dwellings. The 'Fox & Hounds' is a modern name to a Tudor Ale House of obscure origin, and almost next door the 'Cross Keys,' 1470 retains its original arch. The first house on the right side, rebuilt after the 1742 fire, was 'The Three Swans.' *See page* 113.

Photograph lent by Dr. D. Bull

HIS GRACE THE DUKE OF GRAFTON, K.G., ETC.

The Duke of Grafton was President of more local Societies than he could remember, was Chairman of the Stony Stratford Bench and a large landowner. The photograph is from a portrait painted by A. S.

Photograph lent by Dr. D. Bull

COLONEL W. H. BULL, K.H.S., A.D.M.S.

Colonel W. H. Bull commanded for many years the local Bearer Company of the Home Counties Volunteer Infantry Brigade. He was the Brigade's Senior Medical Officer, and jest. Stony Stratford of course was the original home of the phrase " a Cock and Bull Story ", for alongside one another in the High Street were those two hostelries, and in the great coaching days a story told at the one would be capped by the sequel at its neighbour. Of equally ancient lineage and still going strong were the White Horse, founded at least in 1540, the George (1609), King's Head (1640), the Crown (1666), Barley Mow (1667), and the Angel (1693), whilst half-a-dozen others including the Rising Sun, the Cross Keys, the Royal Oak, the Fox and Hounds, and the Plough, dated at least from the middle of the 18th century. Another half-a-dozen were established in the 19th century, four of which were along the Wolverton Road.

By contrast Wolverton, although nearly twice as large, had only three such houses, the Old Radcliffe Arms on Station Hill, and the Hole in the Wall near Glyn Square having been closed down about 1875. The newer ones were the Royal Engineer (Mr. A. E. Pinfold), the Victoria Hotel (Mr. W. H. Tarry), and the North Western Hotel (Mr. C. E. Sanders), all of which were mid-19th century creations. In addition to these there was the Craufurd Arms, opened in July 1907, and of course the Locomotive at Old Wolverton. Wolverton (including Old Wolverton) in fact only had in 1908, eight licensees, including off-licences, compared with Stony Stratford's twenty, whilst even little Loughton had four, which meant one to every 92 of the population as compared with Wolverton's one for every 500.

At Old Stratford there were three public houses, the Falcon (1734), the Black Horse (1820), and the Swan (1800). The first two have since disappeared, but fortunately, we have photographs showing them in the 1900's when the cross-roads there were extremely narrow.

Friday was generally pay-day for all and sundry, and on that day, and on Saturdays the public houses did a roaring trade. There were as yet few restrictions on the sale of alcholic liquors, and the public houses were open from early morning till very late at night continuously. Barmaids could be, and often were, girls who had only just left school, and the ale had a potency which to this generation is unknown. With all these factors, coupled with the absence of such modern alternatives as the cinema, the radio, or television, it is perhaps small wonder that drunkenness was of incredible frequency. One of the pastimes of the youth of the town who were allowed to be up late occasionally was to watch turning out time, with its melancholy procession of reeling men and irate wives who had come to see them home.

This state of affairs not unnaturally produced all sorts of suggestions for reform. The trade itself was anxious to remove this blot upon its inn signs: the church were active in denunciation; magistrates and police equally active in punishing offenders. The trade itself helped to produce licensing laws which made the closing of public houses in the afternoons and at 10.30 or 11 p.m. compulsory. The churches started temperance societies, or Bands of Hope, which did a great deal to warn the young about the evils of drink. Gradually, very gradually, a change came about, and in that change the newly founded Club movement played a great part.

CLUBS

The development of the Clubs is an interesting feature of social life in the neighbourhood. Prior to 1890 the only resort for men and women, and indeed sadly enough for children often, were the public houses, and whilst most of them were respectable houses there were, unfortunately, a few where drunkenness was encouraged to the utmost limits.

The various Licensing Acts helped to correct many of these evils, and they also helped to create an alternative resort, mainly for men, in the form of clubs. The first in this locality was the Stantonbury Working Men's Club which was founded as the result of a meeting held on August 1st, 1893 with Mr. J. Browne in the Chair, and Mr. R. D. Williams as Secretary. The Club still retains the beautifully written early Minute Book, in which Mr. Browne had the very original method of signing the minutes by scrawling his name right across each page. One of the earliest resolutions was that the annual subscriptions should be 2/6, a figure which had remained unchanged for over half a century. In 1894 the club's first premises were opened in Queen Anne Street, and a cleaner was engaged at 4/- per week. Their first order to the brewers was for 1 bottle each of Irish and Scotch whisky, 1 each of rum gin and brandy, two 18-gallon barrels of ale at 1/- a gallon, one 18-gallon barrel at 1/4 a gallon, 9 gallons of stout at 1/4 a gallon, and six dozen pint or half-pint bottles of ales and stout.

On this small cellar and with only a handful of members the club began, but its takings soon amounted to £20 a week, and by 1894 the Committee were bold enough to consider building their own premises in St. James' Street. It is interesting to note that the labours of the Committee were moderately rewarded by a minute which ran " That three pennyworth of refreshments be allowed to each Committeeman on duty ". Opening hours were then 5.30 to 10 p.m., but on Saturdays the times were 12 noon to 10.30 and on Sundays from 11.30 till 2 p.m. and from 6 p.m. to 10 p.m.

The new premises, opened in June 1896, were for several years regarded as a model of what club premises should be in a small town, and in addition to the actual building there was also a quoits bed which proceeded to develop such a generation of quoit players that for a decade they were unbeatable.

Close on its heels followed the Wolverton Social Club, which opened in 1894 at 72, Church Street, and this soon proved such a success that Mr. Walter Thurstans, the Secretary, and his colleagues sought new premises along the Stratford Road, and these were opened in July 1898. It is interesting to record that the gentleman selected to perform the opening ceremony, Mr. B. T. Hall, chose as his method of transport from London his own push-bike, but did not arrive in time, and the opening ceremony was performed by the Chairman, Mr. J. Garside.

About the same time Newport Pagnell had its first Club, and this proved to be so popular that new premises were built on the site of the old " Travellers Rest " and opened in 1902.

New Bradwell was the first place to have two clubs, and the Bradwell Liberal and Progressive Club (now the Progressive Club) challenged from 1906 onwards, the longer established Social Club. The Progressive was fortunate in having not only the normal club amenities, but also fishing, boating and bathing.

The Wolverton Central Club was opened in 1907 and began in its present premises straight away, which showed considerable faith and courage in its promoters.

The Bletchley and Fenny Stratford Club was formed in 1909 in a small cottage in Park Street, and a few years later the first Conservative Clubs in the area came into being, Newport Pagnell and Bletchley leading the way.

It is difficult to assess the full effect of these many clubs on the population of the time : opponents said that they encouraged drinking more than ever, making it respectable, but the club members took the view that social intercourse and amenities were their first aim and the sale of beer a long way second. Whatever our judgment may be, the fact is that by the end of 1910 more than half the male population of this area were members of one club or the other.

All during this period a triangular battle had been going on between the public houses, the clubs, and the temperance movement. The public houses not unnaturally lost a certain amount of their trade to the clubs, but were perhaps losing even more through the activities of the temperance reformers. The club movement was apparently blessed locally by the Church of England, for in 1907 we find that the two clergy of Wolverton St. George's had become club members. This led to a very strong letter in the *Wolverton Express* from the Rev. H. Welch, the Congregational Minister, who not only deplored this support by the clergy of the drink trade, but attacked clubs generally. Referring to one club he wrote : " One has only to see men streaming from the Club on Sunday mornings with jugs in their hands to realise that there is not much difference between these places and public houses ", and he went on to quote that of the club's annual income, £3,075 had come from the sale of drink, and only £130 from that of mineral waters and Bovril. The next edition of the *Wolverton Express* was column high with letters from club supporters, some anonymous, others .signed by Mr. W. Thurstans, the Secretary of the Wolverton Working Men's Social Club, and by E. Taylor of Stony Stratford. All quoted the Bible. Mr. Thurstans pointed out that with their hundreds of members the sale of drink was only just over a shilling a week per member, but somehow the temperance reformers did not regard this as a convincing argument.

Meanwhile plans had been laid for two more additions to Wolverton's array of sociable institutions, for the " Top " Club was now being built, and the Craufurd Arms just opened (July 1907). The latter cost £7,000 to build and its promoters advanced the argument that it would help the temperance cause, since whilst the Manager shared in the profits made on the sale of non-intoxicating beverages, he got no personal advantage by the sale of beers and spirits.

Although there were now 27 ale houses locally, and 6 beer houses, there were only a dozen cases of drunkenness a year, and at the annual licensing sessions it was reported that " Wolverton had a character of great sobriety ".

Yet the amount spent on drink at this period was really high in comparison with other things. In 1907 the national drink bill was £167,000,000, an average expenditure of £18 per family (equivalent to-day to £90). But the next year showed a decrease of £6,000,000, and with the new Licensing Laws, the no-treating order of the first World War, the Band of Hope and other temperance movements, the consumption per head gradually declined, until to-day it is difficult to find either the drunkard or even the merry reveller singing his way home circuitously. In those days they drank twice as much and it was twice as strong, so that it is not surprising that there were quite a number of well recognised topers.

CHAPTER IX

Richman, Poorman, Gypsy, and Tramp

LOCAL FAMILIES

ONE OF THE greatest features of this period was the comparative stability of the population, and with the exception of the railway towns like Wolverton, New Bradwell, and Bletchley, almost every market town and village in North Bucks and South Northants, contained many people who could trace their ancestry back in the same village for hundreds of years. Stony Stratford was a very good case in point, for the Claridges, Barleys, Cowleys, Smiths, Foddys, Godfreys and Holloways could all point to ancestors whose names appear in the Parish Registers when Elizabeth was Queen, and for ought that we know their remote ancestors were here when William the Conqueror was giving orders for the Domesday Book to be drawn up.

Of more recent local ancestry, and much respected generally, were the local nobility or gentry, chief of whom without any question was the autocratic but courteous Seventh Duke of Grafton, who lived at Wakefield Lodge, when he was not at Thetford or in Town. He was born in 1821, so that at the beginning of the 20th century he was already approaching his 80th birthday. He had been Equerry to Queen Victoria or the Prince of Wales for fifty years, a soldier for forty years, (retiring with the rank of General in 1881) and a Duke for twenty years. He had served in the Crimean War, and had been severely wounded in the throat at Inkerman. His whole upbringing had served to make him a lover of feudal pomp, but he also had a great sense of *noblesse oblige*. A glance at his portrait by A. S. Cope, which was presented to him on his 80th birthday, shows the type of face that a Duke ought to own.

He was also an hereditary Knight of the Garter, for every Duke of Grafton had borne this honour, and, as the Duke of Wellington once said, there was " no damned merit about it ! "

Wakefield Lodge was like its owner, truly ducal. The mansion was built about 1730 by the second Duke from the design of W. Kent, and there were subsequent additions to the main pile which were not nearly so admirable and which fortunately have mostly been pulled down by a recent owner. The interior was also what the most fastidious tuft-hunter would have expected. In the Stone Hall, the Dining Room, Drawing Room and several of the bedrooms was a magnificent collection of pictures, mostly of the Duke's ancestors, racing subjects, and conversation pieces. Amongst them were pictures by Stubbs, Cooper, Wouverman, Kneller, Romney, Reynolds, Hoppner, and Vanloo.

The Duke was president of more local Societies than either he or his secretary could remember, he was one of our local magistrates, Chairman of the Bench at Stony Stratford, and without any question the leader in all matters that appertained to South Northants and the continuous portion of Buckinghamshire.

Equally active were his sons, the Earl of Euston, J.P., Lord Alfred Fitzroy, Deputy Lieutenant for Northants, who lived at Whittlebury, and Lt.-Col. Lord Frederick Fitzroy, J.P., and the family reunions at Wakefield Lodge every Christmas were really something worth seeing.

Next perhaps in order of precedence to the old Duke locally was, however, the second Lord Penrhyn, of Wicken Park, who was one of the most discussed peers of his day.

One of the features of the *Wolverton Express* for many years was one headed " Men of the Moment ", and these articles were by no means always of the eulogistic kind. On October 24th, 1902, Lord Penrhyn, who then owned 49,600 acres including a considerable estate at Wicken Park in Northamptonshire, was under review. He was also the owner of important slate quarries at Bethesda in North Wales, where for close on five years there had been a bitter and unhappy strife between him and the slate workers. The men had formed their own Trade Union, which Lord Penrhyn flatly refused to recognise, though he was willing to meet any of his employees individually. The men then " came out on strike "—a phrase then comparatively new in industrial relations—and for five years they stayed out. During that period they were supported by the Bethesda Choir, which toured the country and collected money for the slate workers. The *Wolverton Express* made no comment of its own upon the situation, but quoted an extract from the quarterly report of the General Federation of Trade Unions which was certainly very unfavourable to Lord Penrhyn.

Whatever Wales may have thought of Lord Penrhyn, he was certainly well respected in South Northants, and when he died in 1907 every blind was drawn in Deanshanger and Wicken. The new Lord Penrhyn in his dealing with the slate workers took a vastly different attitude from his father and from his time onwards there has been peace in the Bethesda quarries. He had been M.P. for South Northants from 1895 to 1900, and was not only well known in Wicken, Deanshanger, and Old Stratford, but also very well liked.

Another article in the series " Men of the Moment " dealt with a youngster then new to politics. Winston Spencer Churchill, who had been elected for Oldham in 1900, was evidently well liked by the *Wolverton Express*, for on March 6th, 1903, after reviewing the career of this young man who was then still in his twenties, they said :

> Although a red-hot Conservative, he has proved himself at times a troublesome thorn in the side of his official leaders . . . Few can doubt that, if he lives long enough, and goes on the way in which he has started, that sooner or later, and sooner rather than later, Mr. Churchill will himself gravitate to the Treasury Bench.

But the *Wolverton Express* was not usually given to prophecy, it usually contented itself with a plain, straightforward and extremely objective relation of the news.

We must return to our local gentry, for after the peerage came the local knights and squires usually bracketed together as the " landed gentry ", amongst whom could be reckoned the Lords of the Manor of every village around, some of whom held lands that had been held by their ancestors for hundreds of years. There were the Uthwatts of Great Linford, the Mansels of Cosgrove, the Selby-Lowndes of Winslow, Whaddon, and Calverton, and the Knapps of Little Linford. There was one absentee landlord at least, the ninth Earl of Egmont, who owned much of Calverton. When he died in 1929 people learnt with astonishment and even pleasure that the estates had descended to a distant cousin who was farming on a ranch in Canada.

Added to these were Mr. A. W T. Grant Thorold, J.P., of Cosgrove Hall, Deputy Lieutenant for Lincolnshire, Lt.-Col. W. Duncan, J.P., of Shenley Park, H. S. Leon, J.P., of Bletchley Park, the McCorquodales of Winslow and the Fremantles of Winslow, whose activities are discussed elsewhere in this book.

The death knell of the old order was sounded when Death Duties were first imposed during the Boer War; these were increased in 1907, 1909, and very steeply so during the next half century. The result has been that scarcely a single one of these old estates remains today—they have been taxed out of existence, and instead of the local squire we now have the local officials, growing in number almost every year.

This Edwardian era echoed the last stages of a social hierarchy which had existed from time immemorial. From the days of the Normans onwards the possession of land carried a certain social standing with it, and when land and title were joined then the apex of local society was reached. From the top of this pyramid there broadened out successive layers each of which knew its own place, and kept it. This also applied to the staffs in the great house, for immediately after the ducal or lordly family came the Steward, who, if his lord was interested in politics or either of the Services (as many indeed were), managed the lordly estates, and acted in all ways as the Prime Minister acted under the King.

There followed a descending hierarchy until at the foot in the great house would be the scullery maids or the young "boots". In the stables often the coachman was 'king', and indeed on occasions of state, driving the ducal coach, or even the modest landau, could look as imposing as the Lord Mayor's coachman looks to-day. Sometimes he would be regarded as the equal of the Butler, and was mostly on friendly terms with the housekeeper.

Every year there would be a "Servants Ball" in the ball-room of the great house. The Master would dance with the Housekeeper, the Mistress with the Steward, and the sons and daughters of the house might decorously dance one dance at most with the senior servants.

Fierce and unbending as this antiquated system seemed, yet it was one of great kindliness. Old retainers were usually well looked after, and provided with a cottage and a pension. Not infrequently, the dying lord would leave legacies to the most faithful of his retainers.

It was curiously different in the market towns like Stony Stratford and Newport Pagnell, for here the tradesmen had fought and won for themselves an independence which was valued. But all sought the patronage of the great houses, and just as the merchants of Pall Mall or Bond Street like to boast of their " Royal Warrant ", so our local shopkeepers liked to boast of supplying " The Duke " with this, that, or the other.

At Wolverton and New Bradwell there was little patience or time for these ideas. But even in the Works there were social strata of no mean significance. On entering the Works one became an apprentice, and for seven years one was something less than a man. Once " out of his time," and past his two years as improver or journeyman, the young man theoretically became the equal of all other workmen, yet there was a respect for the foreman that was apparent, whilst the Works Manager was a being almost celestial in his distance from the apprentice. Wolverton and New Bradwell were always willing to doff the metaphorical cap to superior craftsmanship or knowledge, and they had the grand trait of rarely being jealous of the man who had " got on in life." Students who had done well at the Science and Art Institute whilst still apprenticed, and later had left to take up ever increasingly important positions in the engineering world, could count on a warm welcome when they returned to Wolverton, and would be listened to with the greatest respect when they lectured in the building in which they had once been students.

It was a curious world, for whilst on the one hand the legal, military, medical, and diplomatic professions were practically closed to the sons of working men, all other professions and occupations were open to them. The sons of retailers could become great merchants, like " Tommy" Lipton, cycle mechanics could become the heads of great engineering concerns, like Lord Nuffield, and the sons of dockers could become great political leaders, with a seat in the Cabinet, like John Burns, and all these in their turn were honoured by the King. Everything was open to talent, and the Wolverton boy of the 1900's could read Samuel Smiles " *Self Help* " and reflect that the examples which the moralising Samuel could quote of the success that comes through doing more than one is paid for, could be easily outclassed by examples from his own day and time. The young engineer from Wolverton might go anywhere and become anything. And he did. From Calcutta to Chile, from Russia to South Africa, he went with his railway skill and railway character ; he helped to build railways all over the world, or keep them running. For nigh on a century the many republics of South America, the U.S.A., the great

Colonies of Canada, Australia, and New Zealand, came to Wolverton for the men to open out their tremendous territories. Someday some historian-biographer will gather together this great story of Wolverton's contribution to the world. The railways were one of Britain's greatest contributions to civilisation, and in the making of the rolling stock or looking after it, there was no place to beat Wolverton.

An odd sidelight on the period is that whilst it was considered (as indeed it was) a good thing that Wolverton and Stratford men should roam all over the earth, it was not considered right that gypsies from goodness knows where should have the right of roaming here.

GYPSIES

One of the most curious stories in the *Wolverton Express* at this epoch is that of the large band of German gypsies, who, in the October of 1906 took up temporary settlement at Deanshanger. For some days this guttural band of beggars caused no little alarm and complaint in the Northamptonshire village. Finally Superintendent Norman, of Towcester, decided that they must move, and they were asked where they wanted to go to ; the " King of the Gypsies " blandly replied that they were quite happy where they were. The Chief Constable for Northants then ordered them to move on, but was rather handicapped by the knowledge that they could not be deported, but only allowed to move on to some other part of the United Kingdom. After many altercations, the gypsies admitted that if they were going to move anywhere they would move to Scotland, and apparently the Police now received orders (the legality of which was later hotly disputed) to get them moving on their way via Old Stratford and Northampton. The gypsies now pointed out that they could not move, traces were broken, shafts were broken, their animals were sick or had strayed, and so on ; but thirty-five policemen, with various pieces of chain, bits of string, and so on, rendered a sort of first aid to the fantastic collection of vehicles and caught the straying animals. Finally, at a slow walk the colourful and tattered cavalcade moved on through Old Stratford and on to Northampton. Presently the gypsies claimed that their horses were tired, and wanted to pitch camp for that night at Roade, but the police would have none of it. The gypsies were equally determined that they would go no further. The row, while it was on, was exciting, and the gypsy women were more violent than the men. One threw a jug of coffee over P.C. Rose, another struck at Inspector MacLeod with a heavy stick, and when she failed to get her blow home, spat in the Inspector's face. The Police, however, prevailed, and the party continued to Northampton where they arrived about 4 p.m. As they wended their way down Hardingstone Hill they were met by Inspector Allen and a dozen members of the Borough Police Force awaiting to take over from the County Police. That night the gypsies were camped on the muddy Fair Ground at the Cattle Market, and before long the caravans were in a rough circle and half a dozen wig-wam like tents sprang up.

They were no sooner camped than the women and children began begging again, asking for " monish ", or " kleine gelt ", or " ein bischen tabac ", and many there were who gave coppers and other encouragement to the nomadic band. The next day they were escorted to the further boundary of Northampton, where the county police again took over, and so the " raggle-taggle band of gypsies " fade from our view heading towards Scotland, which the gypsies averred was a more generous country than England.

Another tribe of gypsies passed through Stony Stratford in June 1907—on a Sunday morning, and the effect they made may be gathered from the fact that they blew bugles and jingled their tambourines all down the High Street, and had several dancing bears. The Police escorted them to the Old Stratford bridge, where once again the Northampton police took over.

These were, of course, by no means the last of the gypsies, for along the Puxley Road was one of their traditional camping grounds, and even to-day, particularly in the summer months, one can find a caravan or two, with half a dozen horses, encamped peacefully by the wayside.

TRAMPS

In addition to the gypsies, another feature of the time were the tramps. The principal comic papers of the period made much of tramps, and there are few who cannot remember the escapades of " Tired Tim and Weary Willie " in *Chips*, one of the best beloved schoolboy comics of the day. These Tired Tims and Weary Willies could be met in real life, and others too of a more distinguished visage. I can particularly remember one whose name appeared to be John Gorrick, who had a visage not unlike an ancient patriarch. He wore the most tattered collection of clothing I have every seen, and on a string around his waist were several tin cans. He would call at our house, asking for a bit of bread, or a spoonful of tea, and my mother, who believed in helping anybody who needed it, would cheerfully give the desired food. Curiously enough, John Gorrick never asked for more ; he never asked for money or meat, and only once do I remember him asking not for bread, or tea, but for hot water. Childlike I followed him, he stopped in the passage-way leading to our house, sat down, back to wall, and proceeded with his various tins to make himself a pannikin of tea and to munch his bread.

John Gorrick lived in a kind of shepherd's hut in one of the Ryeland fields near Old Wolverton Mill, and made a speciality of getting his drinking water from the spring along Calverton Road—which consequently got the name of Gorrick's Spring. He would then be seen, beanstick in hand, shuffling along to the blacksmith's in Church Street, where, with the smith's permission he would boil a can of tea.

Of course there were tramps and tramps, but old John Gorrick must have been one of the better ones.

Other interesting " characters " who lived at the turn of the century were " The Queen of the Green " and her daughter " Princess Minnie ", who lived in a yard where No. 1, The Green now stands. Both " The Queen " and the " Princess " were dirty and colourful ; they wore flowers in their hats and corsages on all occasions. There was also "Granny Smoke-a-pipe " an incredible old woman, who could often be seen sitting at the base of John Wesley's elm in the Market Square smoking a short clay pipe which had gone black with age. Then there was " Poor Old Joe ", an orange seller, strangely crippled, who lived in a slum then known as Bull's Yard. Every village and town in the neighbourhood had similar oddities of character, they were the flotsam and jetsam of the times, living incredibly wretched lives to our conception, but somehow content with it. Finally there was " Deaf'un ", whom I got to know very well. He was deaf and dumb, and his only occupation was to act as luggage fetcher or carrier for the passengers on the old Tram. For years lads had tormented him by making faces at him or otherwise annoying him, then, at the age of 15 I became the clerk (a very junior one) in the old Tramway Company, and it was to " Deaf'un " that I had to turn on many occasions. He understood the most complicated messages by a combination of lip reading and signs, and would trot off with the truck to Calverton, Deanshanger, anywhere, to fetch luggage. Back safely with the luggage he would be rewarded with a shilling, which he promptly spent at " The Forester's Arms," and spent the next hour or two sleeping it off on the bench in the Tram waiting-room. He, too, lived in a local slum and eventually died just after the first world war. These slums, Parker's Yard, Bull's Yard, White Horse Yard, Hassell's Yard, and so on, were absolutely disgraceful. It was Dr. Maguire who first campaigned for their abolition, and the last of them went in the early 1930's.

I mention these "characters" simply to show that the population of this area at the time did not only include the industrious workman, the careful retailer, the successful professional man, and the landed gentry, with their wives and children, but also persons living in a state of simpleness and dirt which would have been common to our mediaeval ancestors, but which was, as many began to think, decidedly out of place in the twentieth century.

THE WORKHOUSES

One of the greatest blots of the period was the treatment of the unemployed and the aged. It had long been the theory that it was the duty of the family and the parish to look after members who were sick or aged ; and while this worked fairly well in most cases, there were always those elderly infirm people, with neither kith nor kin who found their way to the workhouse. Here, too, provision was made for those who were unemployed or unemployable. By the Act of 1840 parishes were grouped together for better administration, and in this locality there were workhouses at Yardley Gobion, Winslow and Newport Pagnell. It is from the *Wolverton Express* of February 6th 1903 that we come across one of the most pathetic stories of workhouse life in this area. It is headed :

A NEWPORT PAGNELL LOVE STORY
Elopement in Low Life

A remarkable case of elopement by two young lovers from Newport Pagnell Union Workhouse was investigated by the Newport Pagnell Bench on Friday. The Justices present were Mr. J. M. Knapp and Mr. W. R. Chantler. The two lovers were Harry Harper, aged 22, and Annie Cave, aged 18, both inmates of the Union. They were charged with absconding from the Workhouse the previous day and stealing clothes the property of the Union. The prisoners were missed at breakfast time, and a letter was found in the girl's handwriting stating that she and Harper were so much in love with one another that they had decided to run away together and drown themselves.

They appeared in the dock clad in the regulation corduroy and plaid of workhouse dress. These poor beings, apparently in the workhouse because they were absolutely incapable of earning their living, have for a considerable time been making love to one another in the occasional opportunities presented by the rigid discipline of workhouse management. The surreptitious greetings and meetings of these two have troubled the Workhouse Master more than enough, but even he did not experience a sensation of relief when it was discovered that they had eloped. It was impossible for them to have enough money even for a quiet marriage at the Registrar's Office. The young couple, instead of going to the river, began plodding towards London. Their liberty was short-lived, they were brought together the same day and placed in cells at the Police Station.

The Bench, evidently, considering it a very serious case, whether of theft or of clandestine love is not quite clear, sent the man to six weeks hard labour and the woman to fourteen days. Perhaps these spells of prison discipline will inculcate into them habits of industry, and, when they regain their liberty, if they remain faithful to one another, they may start on life's voyage a happy man and woman.

I can find no further trace of the couple, but it is to be hoped that they found some happiness together.

Some workhouses were undeniably hard on their inmates, and even those who wished to be kinder found all sorts of obstacles in the way. In February 1907, for example, there was almost a strike at the Newport Pagnell Union Workhouse, for the tramps, or casuals, as they were called, refused, after a night's hospitality, to break their quota of stones next morning. The reason they gave was that the evening meal of 8 oz. of bread and a pint of water did not give them enough energy for the morning's work—which after all sounds very reasonable. The Master brought the matter before the Newport Pagnell R.D.C. and Board of Guardians, some of whom urged that if instead of water they gave tea or cocoa, like some other institutions, it would increase the numbers. But the majority were somewhat surprised to learn that the supper of plain bread and water had all the force of the Local Government Board's regulations behind it, and that any departure might lead to the Board itself having to pay for the tea or cocoa.

The professional tramps, knew all about the local workhouses, and just what the master was like ; and when winter came, instead of sleeping in a haystack or under a hedge, they would stop one night, or two at the most, at intervening work-houses on the way to their favourite and there settle for the winter and early spring. In addition to the tramps there were also people who for some reason or other could no longer do a good day's work—such for example, was a Mr. Wheeler, who was for many months at the Newport workhouse.

The *Wolverton Express* for June 3rd, 1908 relates that at the meeting of the Newport Pagnell R.D.C. and Board of Guardians one councillor raised the question about an elderly but able-bodied inmate named Wheeler, who, it was though, should be able to get a living outside the House as he was a handy blacksmith. The Master said that Wheeler worked tolerably hard in the House at various jobs, and Mr. T. G. Kirby added that Wheeler might have done very well years ago had it not been for the drink. Mr. J. E. Whiting then said that he would find Wheeler a job if he would sign the Pledge. Wheeler was called in ; we can imagine the scene as he stood there in his rough workhouse corduroys. He was told that Mr. Whiting would find him a job, and the condition. Honest old Wheeler looked at the Board, and said he wanted the job, but " I couldn't do without my beer ". The scene almost parallels several in Dickens. The Board wanting to help the man, the man willing to help—but he " couldn't do without his beer ". Finally a truly British compromise was reached—Wheeler got the job on his promise that he " wouldn't drink too much ". I feel sure that he kept that pledge.

A year later the Board received a curious letter from a Mr. Rakeley, of Germiston, Cardiganshire, asking them to find him a wife. He said he had been to the Union several times, and knew there were women there who would suit him, and he was " lonesum at nites ". The Board wrote back telling him to come and interview the Master.

Winslow Board of Guardians had perhaps an even more interesting case, for in July 1908, James Rhodes, aged 60, approached the Guardians with a request for a black coat and waistcoat, light trousers, a bowler hat, a pair of light boots and a trowel (!) to go courting with. Rhodes, who was an inmate of the Union, had noticed that near the Union was a cottage inhabited by a woman of about 56 years of age, who apparently smiled not unfavourably upon him. He felt that he could not go courting in corduroys and hob-nailed boots.

Photograph lent by Mrs. Staley

A HOUSEHOLD STAFF OF THE 1900'S

The Rev. W. P. Trevelyan, formerly Vicar of Old Wolverton and Rector of Calverton, lived at The Limes, London Road, Stony Stratford, and his staff consisted of two gardeners (Mr. Loveless and Mr. R .Tucker), cook (Mrs. Loveless), lady's maid (Mrs. Trassler), parlourmaid (Miss N. Driscoll) and " tweeny " (Miss Kate ?).

Photograph by J. W. Smith

THE CORONATION OF 1911 AT STONY STRATFORD

Stony Stratford's celebrations included the usual procession all around the town, in which the Fire Brigade, Friendly Societies and schools played a prominent part. Immediately behind the fire brigade engine is the great banner of the Court Prosperity of the Ancient Order of Foresters. See pp. 89 and 145.

BOWLERS AND BEARDS

A group of railway workmen taken inside the Wolverton Works about 1880. See p. 135.

Photographs lent by Mr. E. W. Russell

CAPS AND MOUSTACHES

A group of fitters and engineers taken inside Wolverton Works in 1913. See p. 135.

As for the trowel, he was a jobbing gardener by trade, but bad times and rheumatism had brought him to the workhouse, but with the trowel he would work when he could. The Board could do nothing officially, but had a club round, and James Rhodes courted and won the lady of his choice.

Public opinion from 1900 onwards began to change about these workhouses. Up to then it was true to say that most people thought that if a man wouldn't work he should starve, and that if he couldn't work his relatives or the churches should look after him. But gradually it was realised that the " disgrace " of the workhouse was no fitting end for man or woman who had served their country or family well, and were, through some malady or handicap, unable to work again. By the end of the 1930's much of the worst of the old Workhouse system had passed for ever, and everybody was the better for it.

Looking back it seems as if in the 1900's there were too many tramps, gypsies, and paupers, yet in truth they were only a very tiny part of the population, as were the landed gentry at the other end of the scale ; the great and, indeed, the overwhelming number of our local population were neither rich men, poor men, tramps, or gypsies, they were the steady industrial workers, the farmers and their men, the local retailers and their staffs, with, of course, their wives and families. Over ninety per cent. of the adult population had regular employment or a definite occupation in which they took a pride. The peers, the gypsies and the tramps add considerable colour to our theme, but we must not forget that the essential picture is one of a thriving industrious population that was a credit to England.

CHAPTER X

The Home

MORALS

ONE OF THE GREATEST possible changes, of which no one talked in the 1900's, since it was not considered decent, (and even today is still almost taboo) was birth control, but there is no doubt that it was during this period that there first came into the smaller towns and the villages of this part of England the limitation of families. In the Victorian era, as many local photograph albums testify, it was the fashion to have large families. Queen Victoria herself had had nine children, and what the Good Queen did was good enough to be a pattern for any mother. But in the reign of Edward VII the royal family had shrunk to six, and in a curious way this now became almost the ideal pattern of domestic bliss. Many there were, of course, who did not stop at such trivial figures, and at least one man in Stony Stratford was the father of twenty-two legitimate children, but this was considered to be a little excessive.

Whatever the reasons, families in Wolverton and district began to be smaller with the new century, and possibly this also helped to reduce the infantile mortality rate, which, as has already been mentioned, was over 100 per 1,000 in this area at the beginning of the century, and only 58 per 1,000 in 1908, less than half the mean rate for all England.

This prolific domesticity naturally created great problems for the family budgets of those days, and as a general rule it could be said that the poorer families were those with the most children. It was not that the poorer families bred the fastest, but that in an age when there were no children's allowances, and no abatement of income tax for the married working man (since no working man then paid income tax anyway), the family of four could live nearly twice as well as the family of eight.

Marriage was then something fixed and unalterable. Divorce was unknown, at any rate amongst the wage-earners. To be married was to be coupled for life ; and not only the churches, but the general tone of public opinion supported this point of view. The only escape from an unhappy marriage was suicide, and it is a sobering thought that most of the suicides from drowning at this period were married women.

LABOUR SAVING DEVICES

Apart from this limitation of families and the gradual acceptance of divorce, probably the greatest change in the home was the introduction of labour saving devices, which has gone on apace ever since. Indeed it can be said that the physical work of the housewife has halved in the last fifty years. We have already mentioned the great saving of household work caused by the introduction of indoor lavatories, and the consequent abolition of the daily task of emptying the slops, but it also meant, through the more efficient water supply, a complete abolition of all the pumping and carrying of water that was such a backbreaking business. In 1900, again, all cooking and all heating was done by coal fires. The kitchen range, with its oven, and often a hot water cistern meant a lot of work not only in the carrying of coals, but also the everlasting use of black lead and emery cloth or paper. The black lead was used for preventing the iron grates of the period from rusting, while emery paper was used for cleaning the steel fire irons or fender, which rusted freely when the kettle boiled over. The first change in the traditional method of cooking was by the introduction of gas cookers into Wolverton about 1910 and into Stratford in 1912.

Washing day was then, as now in the villages, a day of intensive effort. Early in the morning the copper fire, often in an outhouse, would be lit, and as soon as the water was boiling the day's wash would begin. Dolly-tubs were used, but not often, the prevailing local method seems to have been the rubbing board with plenty of Sunlight Soap or Hudson's Soap Powder. Many of the local widows became the local washerwomen, ready and willing to give a hand on Mondays to anybody who could afford the eighteenpence for the day's work.

Another development which since 1900 has greatly helped the housewife has been the tremendous improvement in household chemicals and cutlery. In those days cleaning materials were elementary, there were none of the modern detergents, powders, polishes, or creams that are just the thing for the job. The chemist has indeed helped the housewife greatly, and so has the metallurgist, for in 1900 all knives were rustable, and part of the daily chores was the cleaning of knives on a knifeboard made of wood and emery cloth, on to which bath-brick was liberally sprinkled and then the knife rubbed backwards and forwards until it shone as stainless steel does today without any rubbing at all.

Saturday night was the family bath night. Once again the copper would come into use, and the water ladled into a galvanised bath or wooden tub in front of the kitchen fire. In those days of large families the same water would often be used for five or six children in succession, the water being topped up from time to time from the great copper kettle on the hob.

Friday was, of course, market-day, when almost every housewife for miles around would push the pram to Wolverton Market and purchase much of the week's shopping. The Market was then a little distance from the present site (which was then the Schools), and prices, as has been indicated earlier, were such as would astonish the modern generation.

Among the labour saving-devices which became more general at this period was gas light. Gas has been used in the locality since 1838, when the Stony Stratford Gas Light and Coke Company was founded, and gradually its use had spread from the shops to the house, and its extension practically abolished the older oil lamps which added not a little to the day's work. These lamps, which may be seen in a few of our remoter villages, had to be trimmed, cleaned and filled daily, but even with the most careful use they were always a source of danger, since the table lamps of the period were so easily upset by a chance jolt. Hanging lamps were, of course, frequent where there were children, and one of the curious visual effects of the time was the way in which these lamps after being cleaned, trimmed, and lighted, would revolve or sway for a time, making curious shadows round the room.

The new gas lamps had their own danger, and it was not until the coming of electricity that the danger of explosion from the lighting apparatus of the time was reduced to a minimum. In almost every house built in Wolverton at this period, the kitchen, living-room, and bedrooms each had a single gas lamp in the centre of the room, but the parlour or drawing-room had two wall lamps, usually over the mantlepiece. It was to improve the lighting of the room that everybody had a glass overmantle of architectural proportions which, with its many pieces of bevelled glass, reflected the light all over the room. In many of the older houses in Stony Stratford and the villages the Victorian mantelpiece still persisted. The actual mantel-shelf would be heavily draped with cloth, which hung downwards in festoons, and on the shelf itself would be the waxed flowers in glass cases, perhaps a couple of china dogs, and several elaborate photograph frames showing pictures of the family or beloved relatives.

FURNITURE

Furnishings were possibly as comfortable as today, for settees (then called Chesterfields) were just becoming popular in place of the Victorian horsehair sofa, and the upholstered " saddle-bag suite " was almost *de rigeur* for any newlywed. Upstairs, the furniture was oddly unattractive, and had lost much of the solidity of the older types ; and for bedsteads, brass was the latest word. Brass bedsteads, whether double or single were, in fact, the rule—and it seems odd to state that one of the reasons for this was the fact that they were unquestionably hygienic. Bugs simply could not find a comfortable home between brass and iron, and bugs were still to be found in many, many houses in the neighbourhood. In fact it is probably not too much to say that only now was mankind (as exemplified by its members in Wolverton and Stony Stratford) winning its unceasing war against bugs, lice, fleas, and such like things ; and the brass bedsteads helped not a little.

For bedding, the flock mattress was usual, but the best was always a feather bed ; patchwork quilts and coverlets were still to be found in the older families, whilst the eiderdown was just being accepted by those who liked innovations. No mention of the bedroom of this period would be complete without mention of the texts upon the wall. These texts were often beautifully printed, and beautifully framed, for after all Wolverton was the home of fine craftsmen then as now. Some of these texts were extremely comforting, such as : "And underneath are the Everlasting Arms " or " Come unto me all ye that travail and are heavy laden, and I will give you rest " ; but others were most disconcerting, such as " Thou God seest me ", with an inescapable eye printed above the text.

There was also the marble-topped washstand, with its ewer of water and bowl, supplemented by a soap dish and what I think must have been a tooth-brush stand, though tooth-brushes were not exactly common in these days.

The final item of bedroom furniture, the " chamber " under the bed, or the more elaborate night-commode, has already been referred to, but I mention it again only to recall that at Wolverton Market on Fridays there was one salesman, whose name has slipped through the sieve of time, who specialised in selling these " Chamber-sets ". He would start with a Dutch auction, and with a most admirable patter would keep a small crowd intrigued and laughing until he had at last sold another of his " Staffordshire " or " Crown Derby " chamber-sets.

Whilst on the subject of china, every housewife prided herself on her Dinner-set, and Tea-set, for indeed, however short of money the newlyweds might have been when setting up house, someone usually presented the one or the other of these to start the china cupboard.

Another great change in the home is the vast and incredible improvement in medicine. The amount of suffering in the old days from diseases which now only take a short time to cure has almost entirely been forgotten today, and with that suffering there was, of course, the great burden of nursing on the housewife or the elder daughter. In the 1900's two out of every ten people died from consumption, bronchitis, or pneumonia, and one child in every ten died before it was a year old. But in addition to all these indicatable forms of suffering there was the everlasting rheumatism of the aged and the snotty noses of the young. In fact running catarrh was one of the most obvious English complaints, and it was not everybody in those days who used a handkerchief. The average agricultural labourer would in fact have scorned such a feminine frippery when God had provided a finger and thumb for such occasions.

SPITTING AND SWEARING

Certainly one of the changes for the better is in the gradual (but not yet complete) abolition of the habit of spitting. In the days before modern medical science really got going with benzedrine, nasal inhalations, and so on, and before the handkerchief was really a popular article of everyday use, spitting was common and constant. It was a filthy habit, but again one of those last relics of mediaeval, Saxon, or even pre-Adamic customs which survived into the 1900's.

Swearing, too, was common and constant, and shows less signs of disappearance, though its hold is certainly weakening. But Buckinghamshire men swore as they breathed, naturally, and without meaning anything particularly blasting. They swore not to shock or to condemn, but to add parsley to the speech. Everybody had used good round English oaths since time immemorial, and Shakespeare couldn't shock our grandfathers for that reason. But gradually the profane habit is losing its hold, and we no longer have men like the genial and voluble drover whose volleys of unrepeated and unrepeatable oaths could be heard all over the Market Square on Market days.

THE FASHIONS

And now I embark upon a subject which no man can feel happy in writing about—the fashions, and of course, particularly the ladies' fashions. First let us take a glance at the girls and boys.

As can be seen from some of our illustrations, the girls of this period nearly all wore pinafores—long frilly pinafores, which for Sundays were starched to a surprising primness. The dresses underneath were not unusual, being warm and serviceable, but often peeping out from under the dress could be seen the lace edging of the knickers, which were supposed by fond mothers to look " *nice* ". Calico and lace were in extensive use for undergarments at this period.

The boys wore knickerbocker suits of a cloth which was probably warmer, thicker, and more hard-wearing than present-day materials. The coat buttoned high, and over the coat-collar was worn (particularly on Sundays) a wide Eton collar Alternatively the boys wore " sailor fronts ", a charming example of which can be seen in one of our illusrations. Black stockings came up over the knee, as was also the case with the girls, and stout boots finished off the boy's further extremities.

The men wore equally solid materials, cut equally high, but with either a high Gladstone collar or the newer " turn-down " collar (that is when they wore a collar) with a necktie of generous proportions. On work days many wore a scarf, or just the shirt top duly studded. The navvies, the paupers, most of the labourers and farm-workers, wore corduroys, but for

Sundays there was always the neat blue serge or the heavier worsteds.

Ordinary men's clothing was certainly heavy, but even stiffer was the material from which uniforms were made. It is on record that when the Territorials were served out with their new uniforms in 1908 the men could not help being smart on parade as they could not bend in the uniform. Colour-Sergeant W. L. Marsh, at the annual Territorial Dinner of that year caused universal hilarity when he expressed the hope that in future the uniforms " might be a bit more pliable ".

The volunteers, however, could not complain that they had not sufficient variety in headgear, for in the space of a dozen years they had no less than four changes in their head-dress. First there was the shako, a relic of the Crimean War, next there came the helmet with the metal spike, then, under the influence of the Boer War there came in the slouch hat, next came the busby with the plume of the newly established territorials. In addition to these there were the less formal varieties, specimens of which are shown in one of our illustrations depicting some Stratford volunteers in camp at Shorncliffe in 1900.

For civilians likewise there was considerable variety. The cloth cap was a great favourite at this period for week-day wear, and was almost *de rigeur* at work and football matches, as can be seen from our photograph of a group in the Works in 1913 and of the Stony Stratford football team in 1907. But Mr. J. S. Tibbetts was rarely seen without his Homberg, or Mr. Edwin Braggins, the Manager of the Tram, without his silk topper. Mr. Braggins held that he was as important as a Station Master, and since they wore top hats, he did likewise. Mr. C. A. Park also wore a topper daily to work. For Sundays in winter a bowler would be worn, in summer a straw hat, ornamented with club or school colours when possible, but ornamented anyway. But this ornamentation was never quite as decorative as the watch chains of the period. It was every-body's ambition to have a gold watch and chain, and it is surprising the number of both men and women whose ambition in this respect was achieved. But whether the man's watch-chain was of gold or of silver, it was usually ornamented with gold, gold-centred, or just silver, medals. There was scarcely a competition or sport in the neighbourhood for which these medals were not given. Boxing, football, darts, cycling, cricket, billiards, and so on, all rewarded their experts with these rather attractive little shields, and the number and quality of the medals was open and visible proof of the wearer's athletic prowess. Until quite recently these medals were quite jealously guarded, but like military medals, they were not transmissible for wear by a son or nephew, and with the shortage of gold after the first world war (and ever since), the giving of these medals became impossible, and a happy and featureful custom faded away. There was no quicker way to a man's heart than to look at his watch-chain, and to ask politely what the gold medal was for! At the other end of the chain from the watch was frequently a sovereign case, and usually it was not empty. It was not swank, just as the carrying of a pocket book today is not swank; for in an age when money *was* money, this was the safest way of carrying it.

As has been said, the ladies also wore gold watches, often costing as much as a pound each, and presented on the 21st birthday by the father. Most of these watches were of the pin-on type, the wrist-watch not becoming fashionable until after 1910, and were pinned high on the blouse—which brings me in due course to the ladies' fashions.

Looking at the advertisements and fashion sketches in the *Wolverton Express* of the period, one cannot help but come to the conclusion that the feminine form has changed much during the past fifty years, for here are ladies with small heads, smaller waists, long arms and longer skirts, lacey or frilly bodices and picture hats of noble proportions. I am told that this was " The Gibson Girl " type. It may well be, for some carried all before them and others were all behind! I have read and re-read the description that accompanies some of these sketches, and can make nothing of most of them, but here is a fairly intelligible description of the dress of our " cover girl " of 1903 :

Lace and muslin are the order of the day. One of the most popular shades of muslin at the moment is green—the palest grass green. Readers should provide themselves with a good slip bodice and skirt in silk or batiste, and they may then run up muslin overbodices or skirts to match in various colourings. Our illustration shows a full sized collarette of lace set over the shoulders, with a bright green velvet or *panne* waistband drawn through a cut steel or paste buckle. An alternative would be that of flowered pink muslin, heavily encrusted with inexpensive cream-coloured lace. This should be set three times round the skirt, and graduated to the flounce at the back. A further line of insertion should be added down the centre of the skirt. The bodice should be almost hidden by the full shoulder frill of the same lace, and an insertion of the same should be made at the widest part of the sleeve.

As some of our illustrations show, most ladies wore leg-of-mutton sleeves, and skirts which swept the ground, picking up not a little dust and other things.

READING

One of the most significant changes about this period is that around 1900 for the first time in English history the numbers of those who could read and write began to exceed those who could do neither. The Education Act of 1876 had made education compulsory in England and Wales, with provision for school fees in the case of children of poor parents, and by 1900 nearly everybody under 25 could read and write, and possibly a third of those over that age. The immense difference caused by this change can hardly now be realised, but a glimpse of things before the 1876 Education Act is contained in the reminiscences of Mrs. Elizabeth King, of 75, Green Lane, Wolverton, who died at the age of 92 in 1950. She related how, when she was a girl (around the year 1865) during the dinner hour, she would go along to the Locomotive Works to see her father, who was a charge-hand in the Smithy, and every day he would call his little group together to hear the slip of a girl read to them the only available copy of the daily paper.

The new habit of reading, and it was then by no means the underrated accomplishment it is today, was greatly encouraged by the foundation of local libraries. That of the Science and Art Institute was already good of its kind, but a newer one was started at Stony Stratford, and ran for years. At the same time *The Daily News*, *The Daily Chronicle* and *The Daily Mail* were appealing to this new type of readers, and side by side with all this there came a new portent—weekly papers of a type calculated to interest the artisan or housewife. " *Answers* " and " *Tit-Bits* " were now widely read in Wolverton and Stony Stratford, whilst on the lighter side there was an array of papers or periodicals of astonishing interest. I can remember the avidity with which the boys of this period read such varied fare as " *Comic Cuts* ", " *Chips* ", the " *Gem* ", the " *Magnet* ", and " *Chums* ", whilst for the consumption of those who liked broad jokes there were " *Photo Bits* " and " *Ally Sloper* ". The bulbous nosed Alley Sloper was a portent and a symbol of the crude humour of the period ; and neither he, nor the humour he purveyed, survived the first World War.

CHAPTER XI

The End of an Epoch

WE HAVE NOW ALMOST reached the end of our story—but the
final years were to show changes certainly as great as those
which we have already described. In the first place the temper
of European understanding had become very brittle since the
time of the Coronation of King Edward VII, and for years
there had been articles in almost every newspaper in Europe
drawing attention to the growing rivalry and tension between
Britain and Germany. Germany, under Kaiser Wilhelm II had
decided to claim " her place in the sun ", and re-inforced this
claim with the building of a navy that should be at least equal
to that of Britain. Britain replied vigorously, not only on sea,
but on land, and one of the earliest changes was the abolition
of the old Volunteers and the creation of an entirely new
Territorial Army.

THE TERRITORIALS

One of the results of the Boer War had been a very thorough
enquiry into all phases of the British Army, and among those
sections which came in for a good deal of criticism were the
old volunteers. They were unquestionably men of great
patriotism, good marchers and good shots, but as a first line
reserve for a possible European war, much was lacking. Nor
was this criticism confined to high quarters. For half a century
" Punch " had treated the volunteers as a subject for laughter,
and even the *Wolverton Express* had its jokes, for on August
26th, 1904, it reported : " The Bletchley Volunteers were
greatly chagrined at their repeated failure to win the Battalion
cup for smartness, and say their disappointment was brought
about by one of their comrades wearing his socks over the
bottom of his leggings. The rest of the Battalion is now teaching
him to pull up his socks ".

In the new Liberal Government of 1906 Lord Haldane
became War Minister and by the end of 1907 his plans for the

complete abolition of the Volunteers and their replacement by a Territorial Army had received Parliamentary sanction. It was decided that the formal date for the change should be March 31st, 1908. The 1st Bucks Rifle Volunteer Corps now became the Bucks Territorial Battalion attached to the Oxfordshire and Buckinghamshire Light Infantry. The old Nos. 6 and 7 companies at Wolverton became F and G companies, and Capt. L. C. Hawkins took on the dual command. Every volunteer of suitable age (and there were some who were reckoned to be too old for the new force) was invited to join the new territorials and about seventy per cent. took on for a four-year term. The final parade of 250 of the old Volunteers was held in the old Drill Shed, Wolverton, when Major Williams said farewell. For some reason he was the only officer on parade, but Captain Hawkins was present in mufti as a spectator. After the parade the companies formed up in the Stratford Road, and after the Last Post and the Reveille were finally dismissed.

The ambulance Unit at Stony Stratford, still under the command of Capt. C. J. Deyns, M.R.C.S., now became a Field Ambulance Unit of the 2nd South Midland Mounted Brigade (R.A.M.C.), fifty-three men out of sixty-four volunteered for the new Territorial Ambulance Unit. Within a few weeks more enlistments had brought the strength up to 6 officers and 110 men, thus creating the first unit to be at full strength in the whole of the Southern Command.

Meanwhile, Col. W. H. Bull had become Assistant Director of Medical Services and a King's Honorary Surgeon, but still maintained a very considerable interest in the Stony Stratford Ambulance Unit.

Every year there were, as in the Volunteer days, the annual camps. The location varied from Worthing or Shorncliffe to Swanage or Fort Widley. In spite of all efforts to popularise the territorials the Wolverton units were never up to strength and in 1912 lost many of those who signed on in 1908. But the Stony Stratford Ambulance Unit somehow still managed to be at full strength all the time from 1908 to the war years.

In 1914 the new Drill Hall was opened near the Railway Station at Wolverton, and within a few months became a busy centre for the mobilisation of our troops for the first German war.

Meanwhile Stony Stratford and the area around had been the scene of intense military activity, for in 1913 it was decided to hold the annual Army manoeuvres in this region. Great camps were erected, one at Wolverton and the other, even larger, at Stony Stratford, in which were quartered 12,000 men of the 4th Division under Major-General T. D'O. Snow for a period of three weeks. Among the battalions camped in the vicinity were those of the Royal Warwicks, Royal Irish Fusiliers, Royal Dublin Fusiliers, East Lancs., Durham Light Infantry, Gordon Highlanders, Rifle Brigade, Royal Lancs. Fusiliers, South Wales Borderers, Royal Berks, and of course various units of the Royal Field Artillery and the Royal Engineers.

These camps were a sheer delight, not only to the boys of the neighbourhood, but also to the young ladies of all ages. Never before had so many upstanding young men been seen at one time in the district. Everybody welcomed them, and the hospitality extended was really and truly appreciated by the troops. Occasionally it was a little too much, and one of the less impressive memories of the manoeuvres was the use of the regimental hand-truck of a Scottish regiment that was used to bring back to camp men too drunk even to stagger.

With these few exceptions everybody enjoyed the manoeuvres, for they were an exciting change in the dull routine of the area.

Possibly the highest spot was reached when King George V came to Old Stratford to see the troops, for the visit was as unexpected as the uniforms of the foreign military attaches, who provided a feast of colour and smartness usually associated with Ruritanian operas at Drury Lane.

One of the features of these manoeuvres was the use of aeroplanes for reconnaissance work, and indeed the development of this new method of transit and observation was one of the most remarkable achievements of the period. The commercial development of the motor car, and the progress in moving pictures now made these almost ordinary things to the average inhabitant of the area. By the end of 1910 there were over 500 motor vehicles passing through Stony Stratford High Street every week, compared with 1,800 horsed vehicles and 41 traction engines. As for the travelling cinemas or bioscopes scarcely a fair now turned up in the locality without one of these shows. But the aeroplane was still very much of a rarity in these parts.

THE AEROPLANE

When, early in the 1900's, Orville and Wilbur Wright in America made their first hop in a heavier than air machine it made no visible impression on this area, and indeed up to 1909 few were interested even theoretically in aviation. In that year M. Bleriot flew the Channel—a mere twenty miles or so—and the impression on all England was terrific. There were immediate " scares " that England might be invaded or bombed from the air, but the *Wolverton Express* printed an opinion from a very highly placed general at the War Office to show that both were impossible. Within a year even the rustics of the remotest villages around and about were impressed by a thing they had never seen before—an actual aeroplane in flight.

The occasion was engineered by the *Daily Mail*, which in April 1910 offered a prize of £10,000 to the first person to fly from London to Manchester in a heavier than air machine. There were a score of entrants, among them the unknown M. Paulhan from France, and the English Mr. Grahame-White.

The day set for the event was April 27th, but it opened with windy weather, and since in those days a strong puff of wind was likely to blow an aeroplane clean over, all the competitors showed considerable discretion about leaving the starting point.

But at Wolverton and Stony Stratford this was unknown, and from dawn onwards crowds of watchers eagerly scanned the skies from vantage points along the London Road or Stacey Hill. Everybody who had a moment to spare gazed steadily southwards, but hours went by without anything larger than a crow being seen. Round about 6 p.m. the rumour came through that the Frenchman had actually started, and by now everybody was on the look out. About 6.45 p.m. a small speck could be seen coming from the direction of Bletchley. Gradually the speck increased, and soon a curious structure of canvas, wood, and wire was seen. As the rickety Farman bi-plane came over Bradwell and Haversham the pilot could be clearly distinguished, for in those days the pilot sat in the middle of the plane without even a windscreen to protect him. It was the Frenchman ! Within eight or ten minutes the plane had disappeared from view.

Then came the rumour that Grahame-White had left and was hot in pursuit of the Frenchman. Sure enough three-quarters of an hour later, in the failing light, his plane was spotted, and like Paulhan he came directly over Bletchley, Wolverton, and Castlethorpe. Then, a few minutes later he came down at Roade! Somehow or other the fact became known locally in a very few minutes, and almost everybody who had a motor car, or a bicycle and the energy, hared off to Roade, where in a small field Grahame-White had made a perfect landing at 7.55 p.m.

Fifteen minutes later, M. Paulhan descended at Lichfield. The next morning Grahame-White left Roade at 2.48 a.m., making his start by the light of the feeble car lamps of the time. He took a great risk, for it was still dark, and needed two hours till dawn, but there was a chance that by so doing he would pass his sleeping rival at Lichfield, and so be first at Manchester and win the £10,000. But to everybody's bitter disappointment he had to come down at Polesworth, near Tamworth at 4.13 a.m. It was almost the exact minute when M. Paulhan himself started to catch up, and he went on to arrive at Manchester at 5.30 a.m. and win the trophy.

Both flights had been seen by thousands locally, and the phenomenon, like comets in the skies, was discussed for months afterwards in the pubs. and clubs. Even in remote Buckinghamshire it was realised that the time might come when Britain might be invaded from the air, and unwelcome visitors from the Continent shoot at one with revolvers from their planes. But the staggering event soon paled into insignificance with the achievements of the next few years. In April 1911 Mr. Grahame-White flew over the area again, this time in a direct flight from Hendon to Birmingham, but very few turned out to see him. By the end of 1911, a French pilot had remained $14\frac{1}{2}$ hours in the air, covering a distance of 450 miles, another had actually carried twelve passengers in a single plane for a few miles, whilst M. Nieuport in June, 1911, set up the speed record of 80 miles an hour. That year 66 aviators were killed, mostly owing to their undertaking flights in a gusty wind with the result that the machine overturned and came crashing to the ground. In 1910 pilots could be counted in hundreds, in 1912, they could be counted in thousands, by 1916 they could be counted in tens of thousands. It would be interesting to be able to record the name of the first person from this district who actually travelled in an aeroplane; I suspect it would be one of those who in the first world war joined the Royal Air Corps.

The advent of wireless was less spectacular. In 1900 a wireless station had been built at Poldhu, in Cornwall, which passed unnoticed locally. But when in 1910 the Crippen murder case came on everybody was thrilled by reading how his arrest had been brought about by wireless to a ship in mid-ocean. Gradually the scientists brought the wireless within the range of the experimental amateur, and by 1919 there were many locally who had wireless sets on the curious " cats-whisker " principle, and could just get the music or news relayed from 2 L.O.

Meanwhile, in 1911, the Cinema (as distinct from the travelling Bioscope) reached the area. It was at Wolverton that the first cinema theatre was built, and for many years it was known as Barber's Electric Picture Palace. The cheapest seats were then 3d. and the dearest 9d. Films were advertised according to the number of feet they contained, and there was quite a local sensation when, in one of the early programmes there was included the film " Zigomar " of 3,200 feet. Other films shown during those first weeks in December 1911 and January 1912 were " *Outlaw Samaritan* ", " *The Delhi Durbar* " and " *Robin Hood* ". Shortly after this, the enterprising manager, Mr. Moss, introduced variety turns into the middle of the programme, some of which were really outstanding.

In those days, of course, the films were silent, and such sounds as accompanied them came from the pianist. The pianist at Barber's Electric Picture Palace was Mr. Oliver Thorneycroft,[1] and great was the virtuosity he displayed in the choice and execution of themes to accompany a delicate love story, a Wild West thriller, or a Keystone comedy. One night, when " *The Delhi Durbar* " was being shown the film displayed King George V shaking hands with various Indian Princes. Mr. Thorneycroft was not there that evening and his deputy saluted the incident by playing " *Pale Hands I Love Beside the Shalimar* ".

Shortly after this the Electric Picture Palace was opened in Newport Pagnell, and among the first pianists was Mrs. Shedd.

---

[1] Mr. Oliver Thorneycroft is known professionally in the theatrical world as Mr. Olly Aston, and for very many years was Musical Director of the Empire Theatre, Kingston-on-Thames.

Drawing by Mr. C. W. Green

CHURCH STREET CORNER, STONY STRATFORD

The houses in the foreground were erected about 1650, and demolished about 1937. In the background can be seen the old Chancel of St. Giles Church, minus the pinnacles. The Chancel was pulled down in 1927.

Photograph lent by Mr. Compton

The camp at Wolverton during the great Manœuvres of 1913. For a month 12,000 men were camped in the vicinity. See page 141.

Photograph lent by Miss Maguire

FAREWELL TO THE HORSES, 1914.

On the outbreak of the 1914-18 War hundreds of local horses were requisitioned by the War Office. Our photograph shows the first batch of 50 ready to be taken over by the Military in the Market Square in Stony Stratford. On the left may be seen the railing of the cattle pens used on the monthly market days.

THE CORONATION OF 1911

It is perhaps fitting that we should end as we began, with a feast and high holiday. From the Diamond Jubilee of 1897 to the Coronation of King George V in 1911 there had been packed into history more changes than man could have dreamed of, but one thing had not changed, the form and manner of public celebrations. Thus at Stony Stratford, the Coronation of 1911 was almost the same as the Diamond Jubilee of 1897 of the Coronation of 1902. There was the same firing of anvils on the Green at 6 a.m., the same procession around the town, the presentation of souvenirs to the school children, the Sports, the tea for the school children, the meat tea for older inhabitants, the fun with the swings, and the closing down at 10 p.m.

But Stantonbury produced one of the most remarkable displays seen around here for years. Under the vigorous Presidency of Alderman Robert Wylie, with Mr. C. F. Sykes as Treasurer and Mr. A. Beach and Mr. A. S. Jennings, Hon. Secretaries, a remarkable programme was arranged, the centre-piece of which was a National Pageant under the direction of Miss E. Grant. Stantonbury is a small place and its resources are limited, but it put on such a charming programme that over 3,000 spectators were attracted to the place. The day began with the presentation of medals to the children by Mr. Wylie, supported by all the school managers except the Rev. Newman Guest. By 10.30 a.m. the vast procession of the National Pageant started from Kemp's Corner, under the beaming eye of Mr. F. Derricutt who was Chief Marshal—and on horseback too! Unfortunately just as the procession had started Mr. Derricutt's horse fell down with him, and he had to continue to marshal on foot. Following him came the new banner of the National Deposit Friendly Society, and then a succession of carts all of which had been decorated to illustrate some feature of the Empire. The English cart, guarded by the newly formed Boy Scouts, came first, followed by carts representing Scotland, Ireland, Wales, Canada, India, Australia, South Africa, and Newfoundland; then, having exhausted the possibilities of Empire, came carts containing delightful young ladies as Bluebells, Roses, and Prairie Girls, and half a dozen others. Sandwiched between all these were the Bletchley Station Band and the Salvation Army Band. It must have been the most glorious procession all around the town that Stantonbury had ever seen.

In the afternoon the procession processed again, this time with the lovely and dignified Miss Stella Sykes leading the procession as Britannia, and each cart load of revellers in turn as it drew into place in the Recreation Ground proceeded to perform the national dances of the country and sing the traditional songs. There evidently had been some difficulty in determining what were the traditional songs of the colonies, so these were all grouped together and the hymn " O *God Our Help in Ages Past* " sung instead.

Teas were then provided for 1,000 children in the Council Schools, and for the old people in the Assembly Hall. In the evening there were sports and a concert, followed by dancing and fireworks.

It was indeed a very remarkable effort—all from local talent and materials, and its success was such that there had to be an encore three weeks later.

There was one new feature in most of the Coronation celebrations of 1911, and that was the presence of the newly formed Boy Scouts. This fine movement had been founded in 1908 by Lieut-General Sir Robert Baden-Powell, and before long there was a strong troop at Wolverton under the genial influence of " Pa " Holloway. The movement aimed at the promotion of good citizenship and self reliance in the rising generation, and there is no doubt that its moral influence on the youth of the district was great.

Barely had the Coronation finished than the nation was in the throes of a series of strikes, including that of the railwaymen. In 1907 a strike had narrowly been averted by Mr. Lloyd George's proposal to establish conciliation boards, but by 1911 the Amalgamated Society of Railways Servants, the Associated Society of Locomotive Engineers and Firemen, the General Railway Workers Union, and the United Pointsmen and Signalmen's Society, decided to call their men out on strike. On Sunday, August 13th, some of the railwaymen came out. During the preceding three months there had been a drought, and on August 9th local temperatures reached the records of 98° in the shade, and the heat continued. Tempers were brittle. On the Tuesday, the unions issued an ultimatum to the companies to the effect that unless the directors agreed to meet the men there would be a general strike. On Friday,

August 18th, the strike was general, though many of the men at Wolverton declined to take part. A third of the men in the Amalgamated Society of Railway Servants were now on strike, and there was also considerable commotion at McCorquodales.

On Saturday, August 19th the strike was settled. Fortunately there were few of the scenes locally like those in Wales or Scotland or Manchester, where there were hundreds of casualties, but for years afterwards there was great bitterness.

CONCLUSION

In these few pages I have tried to give a faithful picture of the period 1900—1911, but no such sketch would or could be complete unless some assessment is made of the tremendous changes made in men's minds by the new discoveries that were then altering the whole way of life of everbody. In these semi-rural areas, such as Stony Stratford and Wolverton, resistance to change was, of course, more marked than in the more effervescent towns, but even in rural Buckinghamshire the resisters were in a minority compared with those who first gazed in wonder and awe, then became curious about the new machine or gadget or idea, and finally triumphantly mastered it and became its greatest advocates.

The greatest change in men's lives during this period is a debatable subject—possibly it was the introduction of modern sewerage systems and water supplies, with the consequent tremendous reduction in infantile mortality and the improvement in the general health of the community, or it may be in the vast improvements in medicine and surgery that have helped to the same ends ; possibly it was the introduction of gas and electric heating into homes, with all that it meant in terms of man's increasing dominion over cold and damp ; possibly it may have been the advent of motor travel or the aeroplane ; but whatever it was, by 1912 the average inhabitant in this area, and indeed throughout England, was healthier than his father, and had become accustomed to road speeds at least three times as fast as those which were regarded as remarkable at the end of the 19th century.

After delving into the life and ways of our fathers and mothers who lived and flourished in this epoch, 1900—1911, one cannot help but pose the question : " Have things improved during the past forty or fifty years ? " It would be foolish to give either a

" Yes " or " No " to such a question without very careful comparison. First of all let us see what has been lost. Economically, much has been lost, for both the gentry and the middle classes (as exemplified by the clergy of all denominations, etc.) are now living at a lower standard than in 1900's. The sixfold rise in prices over the fifty years has made settled incomes look ridiculous. When the Rev. Newman Guest could complain at Stantonbury that £200 a year was "not much", he was comparing with the older parishes where the parsons received between £250 and £300 a year, and on £300 a year in 1900 one could live tolerably well. But to-day that income (after remembering the expenses that have to be met first) means no room for luxuries or indeed for anything but the sheerest necessities.

Nor does the position seem to have improved with regard to skilled workmen. The 1900 wage of 28s. a week plus bonus would buy more than £7 a week does to-day, and the 1900 wage was free from taxation. Modern wages suffer P.A.Y.E., and the purchases made with today's wages often have a heavy Purchase Tax on them, to say nothing of the extremely heavy taxes on beer, tobacco, entertainments, and so on. In 1900 a working man paid no taxes save the small imposts on beer and such like. Looking back it is astonishing the number of working men in this area who bought their own homes in the period before 1914.

On the other hand the lowest paid workers, and their younger brethren, the juvenile workers, are perhaps better off today. The labourer's 15s. a week in 1900 would be equal to about £4 a week today, but the freedom from taxation in 1900 would certainly be worth at least another £1 a week, so that the lowest economic grades are perhaps a few shillings a week better off, but no more. The lot of widows and orphans has certainly improved over the half century, and so has the relative pay of most of those under 21 years of age.

Fortunately there is less relatively spent on drink today—or shall we say that men and women both are more temperate now than they were 50 years ago ; but on the other hand, the football pools and the cinemas scoop what formerly the public house gathered.

It is a common supposition that in the early part of this century the lot of the sick was somehow chaotic, but almost every doctor ran a " dispensary " whereby for a few pence a week a family could have nearly all the benefits of the present

National Health Scheme, and the Friendly Societies were real friends in times of need. As for the old age pensioners, the 5s. a week of 1908 was worth as much as 30s. a week today, and old age pensioners will draw their own conclusions. Where there has been an improvement is unquestionably in the abolition of the old Poor Law. The old Unions were by no means ideal, and their going is a matter of congratulation.

Thus, economically there has been little advance if any over the 50 years, but without question this is due to the expensive impact of two great world wars, with their shocking waste of men, materials, and money. Had there been no such wars, it is possible that the standards of all would have been vastly higher than they were in 1900.

But if we have not gained economically, have we gained in culture, freedom, or what for a better word we might call goodness?

In culture, almost everybody now can read, but on the other hand the standard of reading seems to have diminished. Daily papers are scarcely better than they were fifty years ago from the point of giving news as news and without tendentious comments. On the other hand, culture through the ear is certainly better, for I do not think anyone would challenge the statement that the B.B.C. news bulletins are better and more informative than anything comparable in the 1900's .Musical appreciation too has inevitably grown, but the number of good amateur players has greatly decreased.

On the side of freedom we have lost much. In the 1900's freedom was real. There were no passports, visas, ration books, registrations with retailers, or limits on what one could spend on food or in travel. There was no conscription. There were very few restrictions on what a man could do, and such as were in force were the age long results of apprentice systems, or similar methods of training designed to protect the public against inferior workmanship or knowledge. Anyone could open a shop or start a business within these limits. The way for new ideas or better service, was straight and open. Everyone believed that everyone would desire to better his own position. The labourer could become a farmer, the industrial worker could become the employer, the shop assistant could become his own master, the errand boy could become a director. Looking around the district it is astonishing the number of names of farmers, industrialists, shopkeepers, etc., who all began at the bottom and worked up. And always this working up seems to have been accompanied by the desire to serve on the local councils, hospital boards, etc., and eventually to become a Justice of the Peace.

In medicine, insurance, or even tinkering, there was the freest field. A doctor might steal another's patients, insurance agents could seek business anywhere, and the tinker, of course, likewise. All classes had one great hope in common, that as the result of their own endeavours their children would enjoy a better life. Education was something that was believed in as the key to progress, the enormous membership of the night-schools at the Science and Art Institute at Wolverton was symbolical of the thirst for knowledge, and there was the absolute certainty that knowledge would in its turn bring industrial or social advancement.

At the back of all this was the feeling of stability which it is now difficult to recapture or even to describe. Prices were stable. The price of coal might fluctuate between winter and summer prices, but it never went above 15s. a ton nor was it cheaper than 12s. a ton. And as with coal so with everything else. There was also the apparent stability of the British Empire, which since Queen Elizabeth's day had steadily grown with the sole exception of the American War of Independence. We were the greatest power in the world; none could, or did, challenge our supremacy on the sea or in the councils.

At home perhaps one of the most significant changes is the replacement of the personal authority of the local Squire or Justice of the Peace by an urban official class. Local government officers, unknown in 1888, now have greater power than the ancient manorial lords. Local councils too have changed, for in the 1900's there were few party contests; today the Conservative and Labour parties run their selected candidates with almost the same fervour with which they fight general elections. All elections now are much politer than they were in the good old days and that certainly is something gained, for the indiscriminate hooliganism and rowdyism of the 1900's had nothing to commend it.

Manners also have improved, there is less spitting in public places and vehicles, public houses no longer provide spittoons and sawdust for throaty customers; the ancient habit of clearing the nose by the use of the fingers has almost passed out; the runny noses of children have dried up after years of sedulous health propaganda, and nits in the hair have disappeared before the advance of cleanliness. There is also more physical politeness in the football crowds—rare indeed are the occasions now when an incensed crowd will do more than boo the referee or a fouling player.

There have also been great gains in the limitation of working hours and the increasing use of machinery. In the 1900's physical strength was often a real asset in employment, today it is the skilled knob-turner or dial-watcher who can command the larger wage. In agriculture, of course, physical dexterity with animals is still an important asset, but the old knowledge of horses has paled before the tractor; today a good farm worker may not know the difference between a pastern and the hock, but he must know what to do on a cold morning when the darned tractor won't start!

Whatever ultimate limbo is tenanted by former horse-ploughmen, they will surely be joined there by hissing ostlers, sludge-cart men and grooms, for the new road age has replaced them by motor mechanics, drivers, and petrol men who can be found in every village. The old bargee, too, seems to be fading away, for road transport has given the canals a draining wound. Railways still hold their place, but not the priority of place which they had for speed and comfort in the 1900's. The twin challenge of the petrol engine on the road and in the air has rocked the great trains badly.

The improvement in road transport helped another vast change, the widening and straightening of our roads. But all this in its turn has brought a great loss in the way of beauty, for the old thatched cottages and winding lanes were much prettier than modern council houses and concreted straight roads, whilst telegraph poles, pylons, advertisement hoardings, and modern garages cannot be said to be beautiful in any sense of the word.

Stability and hope were, perhaps, the key words of the 1900's. It was a proud, confident generation. Had it not been, and had it not had a sense of humour, it would never have survived the challenge of 1914-18, nor have taught us to survive the greater war of 1939-45. One has only to look at the photographs of men going off to the first world war to see this pride, this confidence, and this humour. And I think that all who were young in the 1900's have something of these great British characteristics still in them. There was then a sense of conscious visible greatness, and a great deal of diversity of character, vitality, and gaiety, which have since been lost. There has also been a loss of self-reliance and kindly neighbourliness.

Another thing that appears to have diminished over the half century is that simple faith in the existence of God, as a kindly, just, everlasting Father. The first great war shook this faith to its roots, and the impact of scientific doubt weakened it still more in the following years.

Are we, then, who have wandered and strayed like lost sheep, better or worse than our fathers ? We shall probably never know, for the changes of the last forty years have been so fundamental, and we feel too acutely to be able to judge. But this we do know, that it is something to be able to recall an age that questioned little and believed much.

APPENDIX

"The Ninteen Hundreds"
An update 1951 -1991

AN ERA OF CHANGE

The year of publication of this book, 1951, nationally saw the staging of the major exhibition, The Festival of Britain, in London on the South Bank of the Thames. However, another event twenty years later had a more direct impact on these pages, namely the Decimalisation of the Currency. To assist our readers the conversion rates from Shillings and pence to New pence are given here:

1d - $\frac{1}{2}$p	11d - $4\frac{1}{2}$p	10s - 50p
2d - 1p	12d/1s - 5p	11s - 55p
3d - 1p	2s - 10p	12s - 60p
4d - $1\frac{1}{2}$p	3s - 15p	13s - 65p
5d - 2p	4s - 20p	14s - 70p
6d - $2\frac{1}{2}$p	5s - 25p	15s - 75p
7d - 3p	6s - 30p	16s - 80p
8d - 3p	7s - 35p	17s - 85p
9d - 4p	8s - 40p	18s - 90p
10d - 4p	9s - 45p	19s - 95p
		20s/£1 - 100p

So, taking examples from page 26:
Ale 1s - a gallon equals 5p
Men's shirts at 2/11d is equivalent to $14\frac{1}{2}$p
Petrol at 5d a gallon equals 2p
Dining room suites covered in leather £3.3s.0d = £3.15
8 towels for bedroom 4s = 20p

Sir Frank often relates the events of his youth in "The Nineteen Hundreds" to the publication of the book over forty years later, thus the words "now", "today", "present", "at the moment", "nowadays" and "in the last fifty years" all relate to the year 1951. Sadly however, most of the persons mentioned in the Preface or elsewhere in the text as alive in 1951 are also now a part of the history of the area. The author himself is pictured, aged 4, in the upper illustration facing page 67 - he is standing fourth along from the teacher on the right; whereas his father, Mr W.J. Markham, Secretary of the Football Club is standing fourth from the right in the back row of the upper photograph facing page 79. Whilst referring to photos. it is opportune here to correct the reference in the lower photo. facing page 48: Mr Hawkin's death is related on page 52.

Inevitably there have been changes in institutions, buildings and indeed the very face of the area, particularly since the dramatic development of the New Town of Milton Keynes from the late Sixties onwards, administered by the Milton Keynes Development Corporation and the creation of the Borough of Milton Keynes out of the old Wolverton, Bletchley and Newport Pagnell Urban District Councils and the Newport Pagnell Rural District Council. The designation of a Parliamentary Constituency for Milton Keynes in 1983 meant that it included Newport Pagnell and Olney but not Stony Stratford and Wolverton (reference on page 72). Linslade is now in Bedfordshire South and Milton Keynes is to be divided into two Parliamentary seats - Wolverton & Stony Stratford being in S.W. Milton Keynes.

So-called "free papers" financed from advertising revenue have succeeded the "Wolverton Express" and "Bucks. Standard" (Preface p.xi. & pp 31-2) on which Sir Frank based his researches, yet even the successor to the "Express" merged in 1990 with another paper in its group. Television has outstripped radio as a major medium for information and entertainment.

Both factories of the leading employers at Wolverton (pp.14,19) - the Railway Carriage Works and the Printing Works - operate from reduced factory areas and employ smaller work-forces. Deanshanger Iron Works (p 25) is known as Deanox; Sharp & Wollards of 34 Church Street, Stony Stratford (p.24) has gone but Cowley's Parchment Works at Newport Pagnell still trade.

There have been alterations over the years in local shops (pp. 29,30 & 47). Many individual shops have gone, with the creation of "superstores" and the building of the Milton Keynes City Centre. The wide variety of trades, in Stony Stratford High Street for example, has given way to a concentration of eating-places, estate agents, banks and building societies - few small shops now remain. Cox & Robinson Ltd moved from their traditional location at 75, High Street (which has been converted into an arcade of small units) to 1, Market Square. Odells still trade from 60, High Street; however, Canvin's 1, High Street, Stony Stratford; R.J., Fleming, 17 & 25 High Street, Stony Stratford, premises affected by the Cofferidge Close development; Eady's 39, Church Street, Wolverton, demolished for the Agora Centre; Siwart's 12, Stratford Road, Wolverton and Gurney's of 96-7 Stratford Road, Wolverton - have all ceased trading.

Buildings too have continued to change. Drivers Row (p.14), another name for Young Street - because locomotive drivers on their compulsory stop-over at Wolverton usually found board and lodging there, together with the other Railway-built houses in East Wolverton - Creed and Ledsam Streets and Glyn Square were demolished in the Nineteen sixties. In addition there had been three streets of smaller houses built slightly earlier near the Canal - Cooke, Garnett and Walker Streets, but these had already gone by the mid-1860s as the factory expanded on the northern side of the Stratford Road, to be followed by the demolition of Bury and Gas Streets later in the century for the same reason.

The old Wolverton Congregational Church (p.66) was closed for demolition in 1970. There is now a supermarket on the site, with the new church and church rooms built over it. The Stony Stratford Orphanage Chapel (p.66) is now converted into The Stratfords Restaurant, St Paul's Court, Stony Stratford.

The White Lodge or White House (p.75) opposite 17-21 Wolverton Road, Stony Stratford, was used after the Second World War as an office for the United Counties Bus Company and was eventually demolished to make way for a Bus Station. This in turn has made way for a new housing development. The Scala Cinema was next door to White House.

The Science and Art Institute (p.77) in Church Street, Wolverton, stood empty for some nine years after the building of the Radcliffe School and College of Further Education to the west of the town. Gutted by fire in May 1970 the Institute was demolished in 1971: the site is the Car Park adjacent to the Agora Centre and St. George's Church. The Honours Board, formerly in the Reading Room (p.82) is now at the Milton Keynes Museum of Industry and Rural Life, Stacey Hill Farm, Wolverton and the brass shield (p. 4) recording the names of the Wolverton South African Volunteers is in the County Museum, Church Street, Aylesbury.

The Old School or Market Hall in Creed Street, Wolverton (pp. 80,96) was closed when the Market moved to the Agora Centre, and after refurbishment took on the role of a Travel agency. The Secondary School in Moon Street (p. 80), later redesignated The Grammar School now houses Bushfield Middle School, whilst The Locomotive Inn at Old Wolverton (p.113) was renamed The Galleon.

Finally, in reading "The Nineteen Hundreds" one should recall that the names "Stantonbury", "New Bradwell" and even in the context of this book, the description "Bradwell" are interchangeable, referring to what we know in 1991 as "New Bradwell" and that part of the Bradwell Road "over the hill" in Bradville. Until the advent of the grid-iron system with the development of Milton Keynes, the village of Old Bradwell (now in Milton Keynes terms in the area of "Bradwell") was also more closely-tied to New Bradwell and the villagers would be members of its organisations.

The Society's best thanks are due to Mrs A. Lambert, Miss A. Burman and Mr R. Ayres for their help in compiling the Index and appendix of this book.

INDEX

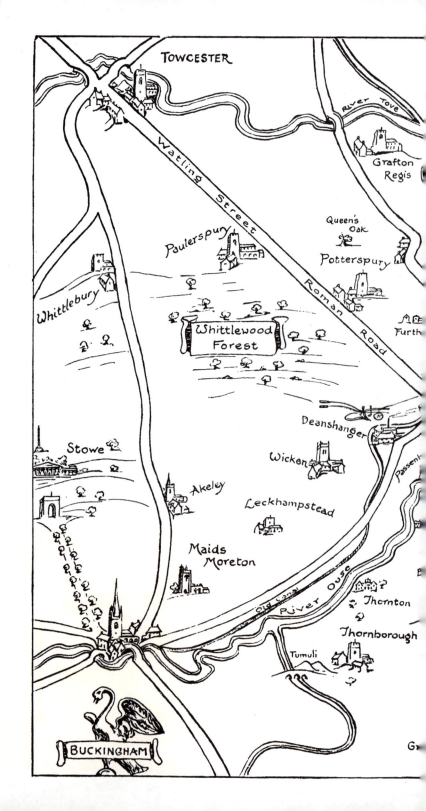